3440
8
£4.50

The Colour Treasury of
Oriental Rugs

Heriz silk carpet. *Iran, nineteenth century. 252 x 192 centimeters. Warp: silk. Woof: silk and cotton. Pile: silk, 5 millimeters high. Density of knotting: 440,000 Turkish knots per square meter. Structure: smooth, thin, pliant, and rather light. Silk Heriz carpets, with their delicate pastel colors and the unusual design that is typical of them, are relatively rare compared to other silk carpets.*

The Colour Treasury of
ORIENTAL RUGS

STEFAN A. MILHOFER

Translated by D. D. Paige

ELSEVIER · PHAIDON

Elsevier-Phaidon
an imprint of PHAIDON PRESS LIMITED
Littlegate House, St Ebbe's Street, Oxford

First published in Great Britain 1976
Originally published as Orientteppiche
© 1971 by Silva Verlag, Zurich

Translation © 1976 Thomas Y Crowell Co, Inc, New York

ISBN 0 7290 0050 8

PRINTED IN BELGIUM
by OFFSET VAN DEN BOSSCHE

Contents

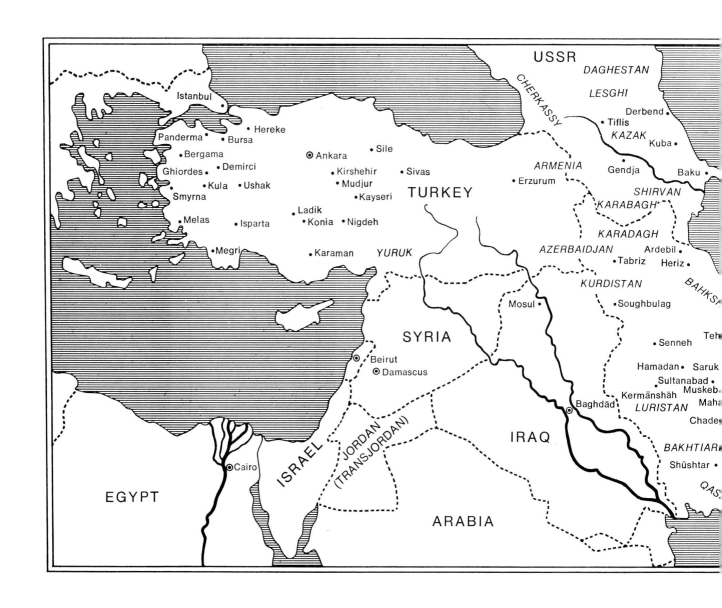

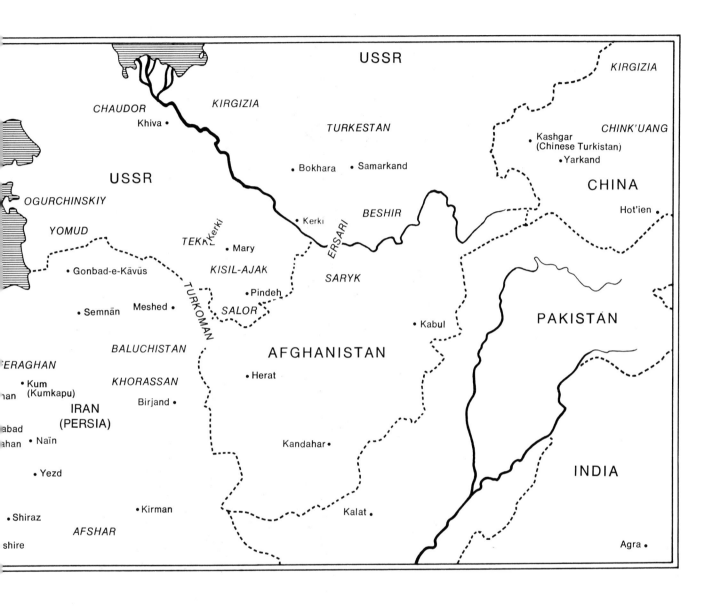

Bidzhov (Bidzhov-Shirvan) rug. *Caucasus, nineteenth century, 204 by 125 centimeters. Warp: wool. Woof: cotton. Pile: wool, 5 millimeters. Density of knotting: 264,000 Turkish knots per square meter. Structure: smooth, tight, pliable. The floral ornaments and leafy arabesques in an ascending movement seem to indicate a kind of prayer rug. The antique style of the "dragon rug" appears in the palmettes, floral arabesques, and serrated leaves.*

Preface

Over the past century, that ancient legacy of the Orient, the rug, has become one of the most important elements of our decorating style. We live with rugs and we are so accustomed to them that we could no longer get along without them. Not only do rugs beautify rooms; they also cushion our walking and afford a pleasant feeling of warmth, thus combining their decorative purpose with utilitarian ends. As a result of the industrial development and prosperity of European countries, interest in Oriental rugs has increased. Thus, even rug factories in Europe and the United States are producing more and more imitation Oriental rugs. Nonetheless, the hand-knotted Oriental rugs are superior by reason of their individuality, quality, and beauty. While they satisfy predetermined needs, they are still real objects of art that enrich our homes and public places by endowing them with a special atmosphere.

Expert knowledge of Oriental rugs—that is, the ability to distinguish the characteristic features of the various kinds, styles, and qualities—is a leisure activity. The practical application of this knowledge contributes both to buying and using such rugs. Not every owner of fine Oriental rugs can become an expert, but the owner of such works of art is glad, nevertheless, to know more about them. Even if one merely has a great passion for Oriental rugs or regards them simply as valuable objects, contemplating them can only enchant one. Knowledge of the essential facts about the laborious weaving of Oriental rugs, their special properties, and their very ancient history is enough to draw us into their magic world.

In this book I deal with all the varieties of Oriental rugs that come from Turkey, the Caucasus, Iran, Central Asia, India, and China. Each kind of rug, whether antique or modern, well- or little-known, is dealt with in a brief description that gives its name and origin as well as its typical pattern, colors, materials, dimensions, construction, type of knot, and the number of knots to the square meter. At the same time, I list the most important dates in the history and development of styles in the rug weaver's art.

I emphasize principally matters of practical

interest such as the investigation of origin, appraisal of value, purchase, and care. Hence, I will take up some of the essentials of the manufacture, the material, and the color of a rug, as well as its designs and ornamental motifs. By way of documentation, I have assembled a rather large selection of each important variety, illustrated by good examples of Oriental rugs that are still available in the market. The illustrations of typical motifs will make it easier to understand the designs. Some of the pictures show how Oriental rugs are made, and for this reason, enable the reader to better visualize and understand this artistic handcraft.

Stefan A. Milhofer

1
The Magic World of the Oriental Rug

Knotted rugs or fragments of them found in archaeological digs have shown that all the techniques of the knot, even the subtlest, as well as the decoration and coloring of rugs had already reached a high degree of perfection during the first millennium B.C. It is all the more surprising that a vast selection of handmade Oriental rugs should appear on the markets of the industrial countries, even in our technological age. Many people are ignorant of the nature of the knotted rug and therefore suppose the modern Oriental rug to be the product of an industrial art. Of course, this is not at all the case, and in the industrially backward countries of the Orient, rugs are knotted by hand just as they have been for centuries, with primitive instruments similar to those used in antiquity. Producers have access to the necessary raw materials and to ill-paid labor for the handcrafting in greater volume than ever before of these artifacts that are so highly prized for trading. The increasing demand in the West demonstrates the great attraction of the Oriental rug. At the same time, however, it encourages mass production, which, depending on the quantity manufactured, supplies only a limited number of quality rugs.

A good Oriental rug is appreciated today above all because it is handmade, uses natural materials, and possesses the ingenuity characteristic of folklore. Hence, people want to live surrounded as much as possible by genuine Oriental rugs, in spite of the rapid advances of depersonalizing technology and the frequent use of substitutes. Since the aura of ancient cultures flows from Oriental rugs by reason of their characteristic patterns, they give our homes a personal tone and atmosphere. What especially enchants us is a perceptible warmth, as well as the rhythm of shapes and colors that please the eye. Certain types of Oriental rugs please us because they correspond to Western styles and gratify our taste. Others, primitive or popular types, with their rare and even eccentric motifs and colors, appeal more to experts, collectors, and enthusiasts who take new pleasure each day in the marvelous effects of the colors and in deciphering the motifs. This is no exaggeration, for the man who is really interested in the works of the rug weaver will learn to recognize and honor in them one of the most elevating and significant realizations of man's creative activity.

The great diversity of Oriental rugs often confuses even the expert. I am thinking not only of the magnificent specimens of the classic art of knotting in Persia, with its system of complicated motifs in two or three superimposed rows, which seems to be so many indecipherable enigmas. But aside from these examples, which are pinnacles of the art, a multitude of rug types with many variations in ornamentation and style has developed over thousands of years, resulting in a miracle of forms and colors. The symphony of exotic hues used in the motifs, often highly suggestive, fixes the eye. We are moved by colors with the brilliance of precious stones and by the charm of the design. How many combinations it took to create such a marvel! The taste for adornment and the inherent artistic sense of the nomadic peoples of Asia led them to invent the rug in order to beautify the interiors of their tents. The splendor of the rulers nurtured this impulse until, with their meditative character and their superior gifts of stylization, the creators brought the art of the rug to its peak in the sixteenth century A.D. The stylistic variety of the rugs, their richness of ornament and composition, recall the constantly changing forms of the kaleidoscope. Although the style, the motifs, and the method of dyeing the wool go back to very old traditions, rugmakers have always made it a matter of principle to give free rein to their gifts of personal invention and to endow each piece with a certain individuality. Thus, rugs of common origin offer an infinite variety of patterns and colors. This wealth of diversity derives first of all from the great distances in Asia. At the same time, the creative talent of the rug-weaving tribes is closely linked to manual work, a fact that makes the identification of many rugs especially difficult. Undoubtedly, knowledge and experience afford a certain confidence, but one soon recognizes that relatively reliable clues as to provenance are afforded less by the ornamentation of the rug than by its colors and the way it is made.

A tribe's way of living, its religion, and the character of the place where it lives—all are evidenced in the naturalistic or abstract ornamentation of its rugs. This mode of expression through the rhythmic repetition of motifs constitutes an unconscious musical event and is, so to speak, the reflection of a soul. Each time, it is accompanied by the sensation of color, which may manifest itself by a contrasting multicolored effect or by a softening of hues. Certain motifs in Persian rugs are like a stylized flower bed or a copse of trees and flowering shrubs. Other effects suggest a vision of nature composed of supernatural plants and flowers, occasionally populated by animals. Many rugs of this kind reflect a heavenly garden, or nature enchanted and poeticized by artistic composition. Still others reflect a splendid garden divided by canals and pools, flower beds, and trees. Such, after all, was the purpose for which the court rug was created—the monarch wanted to have in his palace, even in winter, the reflection of a garden in flower. Many rugs of Persian or Turkish origin present a baroque stylization of the setting, represented by a system of branches interlaced with palmettes and rosettes, which, grouped around a central medallion, created the illusion of continuous movement. Rugs composed in this ancient Oriental style give a tastefully furnished room that classic unity that we have learned to know through Hellenism, the Renaissance, and the baroque. Rugs of another kind, those of folk art, gain their most beautiful effects through their vivid coloring and their original composition. Since the most remote ages the nomadic mountain tribes and the villagers of Asia Minor, the Caucasus, the Iranian plateau, and Central Asia have been creating primarily rugs in which generously conceived and frequently forceful geometric shapes and motifs contain more often than not very ancient symbols or images reminiscent of myth. In this they resemble the motifs of modern painting and attract our attention because involuntarily we attempt to decipher their meaning. The fascinating language of the shapes and the luminosity of the varied coloring imbue these rugs with an enduring modernism. The great Italian and Dutch painters of the fifteenth through the seventeenth centuries, indeed, devoted a prominent place in their works to rugs. Even today, rugs harmonize very well with good decoration of any style whatever.

Most Oriental rugs are decorated either with geometric shapes arranged in the manner of tiles or with floral motifs and arabesques. Identical patterns, of varying size, occur alternately. The rhythmic flow of this kind of decoration is known as continuing relation, which corresponds to the ornamentation of a floor covering, so that these rugs are considered models of the purest style. This being the most ancient style, it is the source from which, over the centuries, all other systems have derived through varying combinations and enrichments. Turkestan, in Central Asia, seems to have been the country of origin of this prototype and of the art of rugmaking, and it was from there, in antiquity, that the Parthians and later the Seljuks carried it into other countries. The progression from the old geometric motifs and ornamentation to floral motifs and arabesques, later changed to medallions, is apparent in the Seljuk

and Ottoman rugs of the first period, which runs from the thirteenth to the sixteenth centuries. The Turkomans of western Turkestan have preserved into our own times, in the purest style, the principle of this ancient decoration for their typical knotted products—that is, Afghan and Bokhara rugs. These sober creations, the decoration of which consists of vertical rows of octagons alternating on a red background, fill a room with serenity and warmth.

Other varieties of rugs, departing from the norm because of the special execution of their design, convey the effect of a picture rather than that of a geometric pattern; for instance, prayer rugs, of which the theme is the various differently shaped prayer niches (mihrab), like the Turkoman's door curtains (hadji, enessi), the surface of which is divided by a cross and filled with little architectural motifs. Rugs with small medallions containing animal and bird motifs also give the impression of being pictures. While this type of picture rug lends itself equally well to wall or floor decoration, the picture rug that, like a tapestry, represents men, animals, or a landscape, can be used only as a wall hanging. Similarly, the finer the weave, the more easily the pictorial themes degenerate into tastelessness.

It is not easy to choose any aesthetic criterion that will enable one to choose among so many different Oriental rugs. Their aesthetic value and their appropriateness to a given place can be determined only by the particular case. Nonetheless, the multitude of styles, motifs, and color combinations makes it possible for everyone to find a rug that suits his taste. The handwoven rug of good quality is always a work of art, the exclusiveness of which endows every room with a personal note—the purpose for which it was originally conceived. It has survived all changes in style down the centuries and all the fashion trends of modern times. Undoubtedly, it will long remain a prized accessory in interior decoration.

When I am asked what essentially constitutes the magic appeal of the Oriental rug, I find it difficult to explain, because it is a matter more of feeling than of intellect. This does not mean that we have to like all rugs indiscriminately, for the mere fact that they are handsome and traditionally decorated is not enough and is no guarantee of artistry, beauty, or quality. The Oriental rug has the peculiar power to transform a room by endowing it with a character of its own often more effectively than a painting or other objects of art could do. It creates a pleasant and enduring atmosphere; the reflection of its colors fills the room by day and night alike, brightening it even during the dreary winter months. In order to meet these demands, however, the Oriental rug must have all the qualities of its race, and first of all, clarity of design and softened, yet brilliant colors in its motifs. Shimmering, durable wool, regular knots, and the structure of the fabric represent the other criteria of a quality rug; the first delights our eyes, while the others guarantee resistance to wear. These questions will be dealt with more fully in the following chapters.

2
2,400 Years of Development in the Art of Rugmaking

The extremely eventful history of the Asian rugmaking tribes, as well as the fragility of the material itself, offers the investigator few clues as to the earliest ages of rugmaking, though such ancient texts as the Bible, the *Iliad,* and the *Odyssey,* in addition to the Greek and Roman historians, frequently mention the soft, many-colored, shining rugs of the Oriental peoples. They speak not only of weaving but also of shaggy and sheared articles that seem to have been rugs of the best wool, made in accordance with the techniques of knotting and napping. As early as the Asian campaigns of Alexander the Great (356–323 B.C.), sovereigns owned rugs "of purple," decorated with animal motifs, which probably originated in the trans-Caspian region of the Sakas or among the ancestors of the Turkomans. It appears from the written sources that the rug was used in the most remote ages, though nothing was said as to how it was made. The generic expression "to weave a rug" is used to refer to a woven rug (*Kilim*) as well as to a knotted one. Arab writers' accounts, though a thousand years more recent, deal in more de-

tailed but less thorough fashion with especially magnificent rugs embroidered with pearls and precious stones. Everything that has been written of the fabulous luxuriousness and splendor of the rugs in the palaces of the ancient Orient, recounted by the Arab narrators, which have so impressed Europeans down to our own time, surely cannot match the artistic worth of Oriental rugs and their wealth of historic and stylistic characteristics.

A more concrete proof of the existence of rugs in ancient times is found in their reproduction in stone and mosaic floors, as well as in wall decorations. These masterpieces, discovered during the excavations of old villas and palaces, have provided a priceless source for the study of the different kinds of rugs of antiquity, their ornamentation, and the evolution of style during the centuries before and after the birth of Christ. Even in the earliest epochs of antiquity, the use of rugs for interior decoration was common; their richness of forms and their fascinating colors represented an inexhaustible source of ideas for the artisans charged with the decoration of

5

floors and walls. The significance of these imitations of rugs is the same as that of the rugs represented in European painting. The experts who have made a scientific study of rugs have profited by these imitations, using them as a basis for their knowledge of styles and periods.

For the nomadic Asian peoples who live in tents, the warmth-giving rug, as well as door curtains and paneling, has represented the major element in the art of decoration since the earliest times. Custom dictated that even in such solid structures as houses, temples, and palaces, the floors and walls should also be covered with rugs. Nonetheless, and especially in the southern regions, the rugs were taken away for the summer and put back for the winter. In order to take their place and thus provide continuity of decoration, walls were decorated and floors were covered with colored stones in mosaic patterns. It is clear that rugs and wall hangings were the usual mode of decorating. The remains found in archaeological digs are full of surprises, and we have many examples of these. One of the most ancient uses of multicolored rugs is confirmed by the discovery of a city more than six thousand years old by a group of English archaeologists in Anatolia—more precisely, in the excavations of Catal-Hüyük—containing fragments of wool fabrics and of wall paintings with geometric motifs corresponding to reproductions of rugs. Another example of one of the earliest imitations of wall rugs by a decoration in multicolored mural mosaic, dating from the third millennium B.C., has been preserved in the colonnade of Uruk. This is probably a faithful reproduction of a fabric wall covering with a diamond-shaped pattern. Little by little, wall painting began to deal with figurative subjects. While borders continued to be decorated with repeated motifs and undulating floral designs, like the borders of rugs, figurative and pictorial representations replaced purely ornamental decoration in the body of the rug. This figurative form of wall covering, in which we see the origin of painted paneling, reached its peak in the Hellenistic era and at the time of the Roman emperors (one is reminded of the famous mural paintings of Pompeii). At the same time, the scenic portrayal of human and animal figures was carried over to floor mosaics. This manner of decorating floors with representational mosaics is similarly due to the influence of the Oriental rug, for the images are generally framed in large geometric forms and distributed in rhythmic sequence over a field surrounded by a border. In this they are like the geometric rugs with animal motifs of the earliest periods, which were decorated with animals framed in squares and octagons.

Mosaic floor coverings are especially significant because they represent the same principles of distribution and decoration as those in Oriental rugs. Many of these marvelous masterpieces of the late Roman period make it possible for us to establish conclusions as to the level of the rugmaking art of the time because the origin of this form of artisanry coincides with the dissemination of the Oriental rug throughout the Roman Empire. Even the technique consisting of composing the images in a mosaic with colored stones is unquestionably similar to that of the knotted rug. The floors of Roman villas and palaces, especially from the second to the fourth centuries A.D., were liberally decorated with mosaics of great artistic merit. Many examples of this art, fortunately, have been preserved, not only in Italy but also along the Rhine, the Moselle, and the Danube, as well as in France, England, Greece, Hungary, and almost everywhere Roman civilization spread. The mosaic artists undoubtedly took their inspiration from rugs originating in the Parthian Empire, which for five hundred years (until A.D. 226) included all the rug-producing regions and which maintained trade relations with Rome. The style of the Roman mosaics is quite varied, just like that of the Oriental rugs. Their source was purely geometric rug patterns, the division of which into squares, diamonds, hexagons, and octagons was generally employed by the mosaic artists as a frame for their representational scenes. There are also many mosaics decorated in stylized floral motifs that recall the Hellenistic conception. The elongated format, the distribution of ornamental motifs within borders in three rows, and the decorative elements of these mosaics are closely linked to those of the Oriental rugs.

Wall and floor coverings whose patterns are derived from the ornamental motifs of Oriental rugs have been found in great quantity in the ruins of ancient Asian cities and virtually all through the areas influenced by Greco-Roman civilization. Many interior decorations found in Egyptian and Assyrian-Babylonian palaces and funerary monuments of the first millennium B.C. seem to have been inspired by contemporary patterns of rugs and wall hangings. The arrangement of fields in equal squares or diamonds is the basis of their ornamentation. This reticulated subdivision of the surface initially gave the basic form to the arrangement of the decoration. The ornamentation of the rug either filled these geometric spaces or used them as a pattern.

A classic example of decoration in the style of a rug is found in the ornamentation of the stone floor of the palace of Sennacherib (705–681 B.C.) in Nineveh. The decoration of this "stone rug," done in bas-relief, is composed of a series of squares. The edges of the squares, adorned with rosettes, enclose the main motif in a star composed of four lotus flowers and four lotus buds. This central motif is surrounded by a broad border decorated by sinuous floral patterns from which lotus flowers and buds are suspended. A knotted rug of the fifth century B.C. found in Pazyryk, with almost identical central ornamentation, proves that this work is in fact a reproduction of a rug pattern of that period.

As the numerous remains of floor, wall, and ceiling decorations show, the decorative art of antiquity was based above all on the division of reticulated and honeycomb surfaces into geometric forms. These simple shapes were decorated like frames and filled either with floral ornaments or with figures of animals and fabulous beings. Analysis of the style of these decorations in antiquity has led to the belief that we are dealing with an art form that originated largely from the conceptions of the age-old art of rugmaking and its great practical and cultural importance for the people of the Orient. For years there was no evidence to support this hypothesis, for there existed no rug specimen earlier than those of the Seljuks, dating from the thirteenth century A.D.

Then, through a remarkable and unanticipated coincidence, overwhelming and irrefutable proof came to light. In 1949, among the Scythian royal tombs in the Altai region, near Outer Mongolia, Soviet archaeologists found a number of specimens of textile artisanry of great artistic value, as well as a handknotted rug, all of which constituted part of the treasures buried with the Scythian kings during the fifth and fourth centuries B.C. These fabrics had been preserved for 2,400 years in the eternal ice formed in the wooden mortuary chambers as a result of the rapid freezing of water seeping in. Consequently, the extremely fragile contents of the tombs had been amazingly well preserved. What is especially interesting is the handknotted rug found in a tomb so ancient (now world-famous); it is sensational in itself, for it would be a miracle to find another such rug, to say nothing of an older one. What is even more surprising is

7

the relatively intact state of this rug, which constitutes a remarkable work of art both in its technical perfection and its design. The tight, dense pile—360,000 knots to the square meter—is made with Turkish (Ghiordes) knots. Consequently, it has a fine, smooth texture, formed by the warp and woof of wool twisted in a particularly delicate manner. In a band 10 centimeters wide there are approximately 120 chain links. In order to bring out the motifs and the ornaments of the detailed design of this rug, the woolen pile was sheared to 2 millimeters. If one reflects that work of this kind is itself exceptional in the history of rug-knotting, one can form some idea of the importance of this rug made 2,400 years ago. The stage of refinement bordering on technical perfection represented by this specimen compels us to assume the existence of a very long evolutionary process, and thus places the origin of rug-making several centuries earlier. Moreover, the Pazyryk rug, which might have been a fluke resulting from especially favorable circumstances, is not the only evidence; fragments of another unusually fine rug, also found in an "ice tomb" near Bashadar, in the Altai region, attest to the high degree of perfection of the knotting technique in remote antiquity. Examination of these fragments has made it possible to establish a density of 700,000 Persian (Senneh) knots per square meter for this rug; such a density of knots is unusual and has only rarely been exceeded. The fine texture of the few fragments found enables us not only to speculate as to the great age of this work of art but also indicates that such masterpieces could have been created only sporadically over the centuries. In view of the primitive and unstable conditions of the period, it was much more difficult at that time to make the knots than it is today, when chiefly felt and woven rugs (Kilim) are made for daily use. The work of knotting was difficult not because of the

primitive equipment but solely because it was handwork, requiring a great deal of time, which might have to be stretched out over years because of the interruptions caused by other necessary activities. Even the finest of the knotted rugs, like the woven ones, were worked on a very simple device, consisting of two beams to which was attached a warp stretched horizontally on the floor and attached to blocks of wood planted in the ground. This rudimentary weaving and knitting loom is still used today by the rural and nomadic tribes of Asia (see illustrations on pages 99 and 103). The famous Bokhara rugs, with their very tight knotting, are made by Turkomans in the same way. Possibly the producers of the Pazyryk and Bashadar rugs were the Central Asian tribes who were the ancestors of the Turkomans.

Various hypotheses indicate that Media or Persia was the area where the technique of knotting in general and of the knotted rug in particular originated. It is believed that royal manufactories were already functioning under the dynasty of the Achaemenides—a very tempting supposition. But in fact, if one is to judge by the stage of development of the fragments found in the Altai, the origin of the knotted rug must be traced back to an earlier period. This art was born when primitive nomadic tribes enriched ordinary fabric with additional bits of wool knotted on the warp in order to insulate their tents. Thus, by imitating animals' fur, they provided themselves with a thicker and more tufted covering for the earthen floor. These first steps toward the knotted rug probably date back to the third or even the fourth millennium B.C. The refinement of knotting methods and the ornamentation of rugs with stripes or squares of natural-colored wool logically developed from this. The next step in the evolution was to insert primitive patterns, depictions of animals and men, which, moreover, are frequently found on many other utilitarian objects among the prehistoric nomads.

The Pazyryk rug and the Bashadar fragments dating from the fifth century B.C. prove by their delicacy and their highly developed technique that they are certainly not among the oldest examples of knotting; they are merely the most ancient specimens preserved to us from those centuries during which rugs of this style were known in the Near East and enjoyed a favor equaled by their influence on other branches of artisanry. The question arises whether the rugs indeed served as models for artisans or whether, on the contrary, floor and wall ornamentation provided inspiration for the rugmakers. The question arose only when it was found that the central motif of the Pazyryk rug corresponded remarkably with the ornamentation of the stone floor of the palace of Nineveh, now Kuyunjik, created two hundred years before the rug.

Since the origin of the knotted rug goes back to earliest antiquity, as is proved by the degree of its development and technical sophistication, we have almost certain proof for the thesis that knotted works similar to the Pazyryk rug in their ornamentation were created even earlier. When one takes into account the Orientals' ageless attachment to all ornamental motifs handed down from generation to generation, one may suppose that, similarly, this design could have existed for some time and served as a model to the artisan.

Summarizing the artistic evolution of the Oriental rug, we can begin with the ornamentation of the Pazyryk rug, taking it as the oldest extant example of this art. The rug measures 200 by 190 centimeters, so it is approximately square. The conception and the distribution of its ornamentation give the impression of the preclassic rather than the archaic, and indicate a pronounced structural talent in its designer. The

rug's relatively small central motif is surrounded by a total of eleven borders: two wide borders decorated in the style of a frieze, three narrow ones, and six fine stripes. The central motif is covered checkerboard fashion by twenty-four (6 × 4) square motifs. Each square motif, isolated and framed in a fine stripe, contains four flowers in cross form and four spear-shaped leaves arranged diagonally, the whole forming a star. The inner border is decorated in the style of a frieze with a procession of grazing elk, and the main border with a procession of horsemen going in a direction opposite to that of the elk. The narrow borders contain a succession of small octagonal cartouches filled with griffins or star-shaped flowers. These borders that we have described are separated by the six fine-stripe borders. The distribution of figures and motifs is probably based on religious imagery. From the point of view of style, the ornamentation of the Pazyryk rug, though it is not overburdened, consists of floral, figurative, and geometric forms used in combination. The ornamentation is rich in motifs and yet balanced in proportion. It shows evidence of maturity and is classic in its artistic conception. For all these reasons this rug can be compared with the finest works of art of antiquity. Its radiant colors, more or less recognizable as tones of dark or light red, light blue, green, yellow, and brown, are the product of vegetable dyes.

To ask, as people often have, what tribe created the Pazyryk rug in particular or knotted rugs in antiquity in general is to look for a needle in a haystack. Among the many Asian tribes, as well as the multitude of heterogeneous peoples in the Iranian sphere of influence, the groups that made knotted rugs in addition to felt and woven rugs (*Kilim*) were certainly not isolated. Most of these people had always bred livestock and engaged in nomadic or seminomadic pasturage. Of necessity these occupations played a more important part than agriculture because of the arid steppes on which the tribes lived. Experience has shown right down to the present that nomadic herdsmen enjoy all the natural conditions to make them the creators of the art of knotting rugs. That their way of living and their primitive instruments do not preclude a very high degree of artistic skill is still demonstrated in our own time by the special quality, delicacy, and beauty of the ornaments and colors of many of the products of the nomadic Turkomans, Baluchis, Kurds, Kashgari, and other tribes. We may regard a number of tribes of southern Siberia, Central Asia, Iran, the Caucasus, and Asia Minor as the makers of knotted rugs like that of Pazyryk, as early as the first millennium B.C. Popular art is always the basis of the art of high civilizations. The kind of knot used is in no way decisive as to the origin of a rug, for the peoples I have mentioned have always used the Turkish knot or the Persian knot indiscriminately. Nor is it legitimate to draw conclusions as to the provenance of a rug on the basis of its ornamentation, for since the earliest times decorated objects have always been carried over great distances as trading goods, war booty, and gifts. Thereafter they have been incorporated into the decoration of dress, of objects for daily use, and of rugs in a given region. Such migrations of motifs and images have occurred throughout the world. Take, for example, the multitude of Hellenistic influences on the heart of Asia, or the influence of Oriental art forms on Europe. Even the generous use of vegetable dyes cannot be a clue as to the origin of the Pazyryk rug, for there are splendid colors in the felt rugs undoubtedly produced by the nomadic tribes of the Altai at the same period. The sole test that might verify the origin is the style and pattern of the ornamentation. This style, in fact,

is so simple and uniform as far as the distribution of motifs is concerned, both in the knotted rugs and in the felt rugs of the Altai graves, that it can be regarded as characteristic of this period. As I have already pointed out, it constituted the base, into the sixteenth century A.D., of all pattern arrangements in the Turkish rugs of Asia Minor. The Afghan and Bokhara rugs of the Turkomans of Central Asia have retained these patterns even into the present. The Bokhara rugs are the closest to the Pazyryk rug's style, especially in the arrangement of the decoration of the central field of the Pazyryk rug, which, with its surrounding narrow border containing a row of little octagons, presages and prefigures the ornamentation of the Bokhara rug. As for the ethnographic origin of the art of rug tying, which is at least three thousand years old, there is no concrete proof. It is beyond dispute that the tying art of our millennium was practiced and spread abroad by the Turkish people of Asia, for this art has taken root down to the present wherever Turkish peoples or tribes predominate. Consequently, one may assume that the ancestors of the Turkish peoples produced the rugs of antiquity. Long before they instituted their own states, these ancestors of the Turks, under various names of warlike tribes of herdsmen, established themselves among the heterogeneous peoples of the countries in which they still live today: eastern and western Turkestan and certain areas of the Caucasus, Anatolia, southern Siberia, and Iran, in particular. Nonetheless, in spite of a certain linguistic affinity and all kinds of interbreeding, the Turkish peoples have no ethnic connection with the Mongol group, though superficial confusion frequently leads to the contrary assumption. The differences of physiognomy and language between these two groups may be likened to the differences between the Swedes and the Spanish.

3
Artistic Value

The discovery of the important artistic value of Oriental rugs is not recent. As early as the fourteenth century, in fact, the Italian painters gave them a very prominent position in their pictures. In the centuries that followed, they are represented as playing an important part in the life of the period. Rugs were attributes of royalty; they enhanced the significance of religious settings and were much esteemed as luxury goods in commerce. The great masters of the seventeenth century used Persian rugs as backgrounds for their paintings, while the Dutch painters, probably under the vivid impression of some particularly splendid examples, preferred varieties of rugs from Asia Minor and the Caucasus.

To this quotation from Arthur Upham Pope, the famous Orientalist, one must add that, on the basis of these reproductions of Oriental rugs in European painting, and particularly as the result of the example of F. M. Martin (*History of the Oriental Rug before 1800*), scholars began to study the Oriental rugs that had made

their way to Europe and to write their history. These studies began about eighty-five years ago, but they will require still more time and patience.

The artistic development of the Oriental rug did not follow a straight line in the 2,000 years between the creation of the Pazyryk rug and the height of the art in the sixteenth century. As in all arts, this development had periods of brilliance followed by others of prolonged stagnation that have left us no specimens of the knotted rug. In spite of political and economic crises, the art of rug tying was practiced uninterruptedly by the nomadic tribes, which, though employing traditional themes for centuries, varied and developed them, thus providing a basic stock for the designers of the royal and other manufactories. The development of ornamentation in the style of the Oriental rug attests to the continuity of the art of rug tying as an expression of folk art. Here a brief explanation is necessary.

Thus far hardly any attention has been paid to the felt rugs found in the Altai tombs, for they were eclipsed by the importance of the

Pazyryk rug, which is knotted; and yet these products of the nomads' art, rich in colors and dating from the fifth and fourth centuries B.C. show the basic pattern that characterizes the style of rugmaking and already hint at the principles of ornamentation that we will encounter again in future developments. In its fields conceived in the manner of a frieze, framed by decorated borders, a large wall rug of Pazyryk shows the same religious scene six times, portrayed in naturalistic fashion—a goddess on her throne offers the flowering tree of life to a horseman. This felt hanging is a good example of the fact that it was not always the borders of a rug but often its central field alone that was filled with figurative motifs. According to written sources, the different geometric divisions of the central field of a knotted rug were also ornamented with figurative scenes. Small felt rugs, saddle cloths of the period, present almost all the varieties of simple patterns of Oriental rugs. In one the field is divided into diamonds. These diamonds are composed of diagonal bands; at the points of intersection and within the fields of these diamonds there are rosettes. In another felt rug the pattern consists of rosettes in a staggered arrangement with clematis leaves. This arrangement of the rug's ornamentation, still employed today, is derived from the arrangement in diamonds with rosettes, but without the diagonal bands. On a third felt rug we find the rare pattern of ascending motifs. Two kinds of palmettes, arranged in staggered rows, form a close scalloped-style pattern. The smallest of the felt rugs has a grouped order of ornaments. An elongated rectangle in the middle of the field encloses highly stylized tendrils ornamented with flowers. The borders of the felt rugs are ornamented with S-shaped or spiral tendrils, flowers and leaves in alternating arrangement, and

flame-shaped figures in Kirghiz style. If we consider the many other ornaments and decorations on the various objects of nomad art of this period, we can see that all the artistic material necessary to the development of the art of rug knotting was at hand. These ornaments and patterns are described in many illustrated publications by Russian archaeologists both present and past.

Our best materials for studying the next period in the development of the art are the fragments of textiles found in eastern Turkestan by the Turfan expedition; they were preserved by the sand that buried the tombs of the ancient cities of Loûlan, Niya, and Astana. These are fragments of wool rugs made with the Turkish knot, woven wool rugs (Kilim), and silk fabrics dating from the third and second centuries B.C. The fragments of knotted rugs are ornamented only with motifs of multicolored diamonds and spiral leaves, while the Kilim have various floral motifs. The highly developed patterns of the silk fabrics are especially significant. These patterns have bands in the form of tendrils from which flowers hang. The bands contain fabulous birds and animals in two colors. A characteristic pattern consists of staggered disks that contain two birds facing and fighting each other. Another pattern has tendrils with flowers in spiral rolls. These decorative themes play an important part in the development of the knotted rug, for they seem to show the transition to the standard patterns of the Seljuk rugs, as well as to the thirteenth- and fourteenth-century geometric rugs of Asia Minor with animal subjects. A fourth pattern in a silk material from eastern Turkestan is equally important. This pattern consists of flower rosettes alternating in a staggered arrangement with four flowers arranged in the shape of a cross. In this design we find for the first time the alternating staggered arrangement of two different subjects, which, in the fifteenth century, even for the Ottoman rugs of the first period, was to lead to the development of the arabesque. Even today the standard, well-known design of the Tekke (Bokhara) rugs preserves this very ancient ornamentation in its rosette octagon and the diamond of cruciform flowers that accompanies it. We do not know whether the designs of the silks were used in rug knotting during the Middle Ages, but to judge from the examples of later periods, the probability exists. These silks were probably an autochthonous creation of the people of the Turkestan oases, although influenced by Chinese silks. Their designs are indisputably marked by the more ancient ornamentation of the felt rugs made by the nomadic tribes.

The history of the art of rug tying as illustrated by still existing specimens begins only with the magnificent rug production of the Seljuks. This beginning is in itself a golden age, a period of expansion that endured. The rug production of the Seljuks and the Ottomans in Asia Minor, as well as that of the Mamelukes in Egypt from the twelfth to the sixteenth centuries, which was marked by a great number of variations, may be considered the classic period of the art of rug tying. It reached its culmination in Persia, where, during the sixteenth and seventeenth centuries, the royal rug manufactories of Tabriz, Ispahan, Kashan, Herat, and Kirman created rugs that were artistically sumptuous and answered the most demanding requirements.

Masterpieces of the period of classic flowering in the art are preserved as unique treasures in all the major museums of the world. They present an infinite number of systems of design expressed in the varied division of patterns and the individuality of ornamentation. Only one

familiar with the evolution of this design from antiquity to the golden age can resolve the "enigma" of its double and triple combinations of independent projects. These projects are based in general on one of the original divisions formed in the pattern by geometric shapes (squares, lozenges, hexagons, octagons) that produce a reticular arrangement of the rug's field. The decorative elements are placed at the points of intersection of the tracery and in its fields. If, on the other hand, one omits the dividing lines, all that is left in the field is rows of staggered ornaments, which represent the pure, coordinated design. Geometry supplied a structural basis for a host of ways of combining the subordinating division of the pattern. Gifted designers replaced the simple lines of the geometric divisions with curved, undulating, sinuous lines. Thus, through rhythmic repetition, they created a decorative ornamentation composed of tendrils, leaves, flowers, and buds—the arabesque, an ornamental motif that, to the Westerner, seems as impenetrable as a virgin forest. Two or three of these patterns, each of which is constructed on a different geometric basis but which is in itself complete and autonomous, are copied one over another and assembled in strata. On the drawing that serves as a model to the artisans, the autonomous stages are shown already merged in a single pattern. The only way of distinguishing the intertwined, ramified systems of design was through differences of color. Among the tendrils, flowers, and arabesques, the designers inserted the motif of the cloud band (*tschi*), vases, people, and animals, as well as hunting scenes and animal fights. In this way the designers created multiple variations that are works of art in their imagery and color. Pope, commenting on the fugal form of these combined projects, wrote: "The conception and composition require as much intellectual effort as the viewer must exert in order to recognize them." Thorough studies by Charles Grant Ellis and Kurt Erdmann have contributed to the decipherment of the design systems of the sixteenth century. These systems can be broken down according to their tiered elements into superimposed layers if they are traced separately on transparent paper. The first layer of the motif is based on the arrangement in diamonds, the second is based on the square, and the third is based on the hexagon. If one superimposes the traced designs on a pane of glass illuminated from below, it appears that each system of design complements the others and that each composition presents new variations on a multilayered system of patterns. The illustrators of Persian books created similar complicated designs that could be employed in the creation of court rugs as well. The works of art created earlier by the Seljuks in Persia and Asia Minor served as models for the very finest creations of the illustrators of Persian books. For in the Seljuk period independent coordinated and subordinated systems of design were used for the first time by different arts. The Seljuks' minia-

tures, works in plaster, pottery decoration, engraving on metal, and in particular, the motifs of their fabrics and rugs bear an amazing resemblance to the models of Persian and Ottoman rug tying of the golden age. The Seljuks' rug designs in particular, so rich in variations, afforded many examples of perfect ornamentation of different combinations. The fact that, of the eighteen existing Seljuk rugs dating from the thirteenth century, sixteen have totally different motifs, demonstrates the astonishing wealth of their ornamentation. Even the well-known ornamentation of the Persian rugs of the classic period, with their concentric arrangement of the medallion in the center of the field and quarters of the medallion placed in the corners, is derived from a Seljuk model through the staggered alignment of the two motifs. This type of ornamentation divided by medallions is simply a detail taken from the motif enlarged beyond its dimensions, variations of which are used to fill the entire field of the rug.

The rugs characteristic of various regions, cities, and nomadic tribes will be dealt with in Chapters 10 to 14.

4

The Collector and the Amateur

Ever since the Renaissance, many Westerners have been keenly interested in the Oriental rug. They have made every effort to obtain rare, if not unique, specimens. According to some accounts, Roman aristocrats of Caesar's time collected these precious objects in large numbers. Even at that time it was possible to obtain such rugs, not only through the intermediary of the Roman legions stationed in Oriental countries but also through the busy caravan trade with the Far Eastern countries along the "silk road" that led to China. Splendid mosaic floors of the late Roman period have obviously been influenced artistically by the Oriental rug. In modern times, not only the church and the diplomatic corps but also rich merchants and artists have become amateurs, experts, and collectors of Oriental rugs.

In the beginning, these richly colored objects were highly valued and treated with great care, being used almost exclusively as rugs or hangings until the eighteenth century. Stanley Reed, expert and collector, wrote in a recent book:

Lovers of rugs ought to treat their rugs with the greatest care and caution possible. Rugs deserve to be much better taken care of than is the rule. If one is aware that a knotted rug of average size represents two years' work by one person, then it is inconceivable that one would walk on it with shoes.

It is a fact that no other object of art can be used with as little care as rugs created as floor coverings. Orientals walk barefoot on their rugs. To them the rug represents not only a work of art made by hand with infinite pains but at the same time the essential object in the furnishing of the home. Reed's observation might refer to particular specimens—rare, ancient, interesting from the point of view of art history, specimens that are in some intrinsic way of finer quality and more delicate structure. Therefore they require more care than many new knotted rugs of thicker quality and more solid structure, which are more easily replaced. One must be an expert in order to know what kind of rug represents a precious piece that ought not to be used excessively.

15

Over the past eighty years the growing interest in Oriental rugs and the close study of their varieties have produced a great number of experts who have realized that the artistic value of certain knotted rugs equals that of other art objects. The number of enthusiasts and collectors has not ceased to grow. Recognizing that these products contained the artistic expression of various countries and peoples, the amateur discovered through experience special values—chiefly, the fascination exerted by the styles of each group of rugs, but also the rarity and individuality of some examples. Among the common types of almost every variety of rug there are rare variations or exceptional specimens of great artistic value. There are also rare kinds of rugs which have added value when they appear on the market. It is unnecessary to give examples in this chapter because we will deal with them later. From time to time we encounter examples of a more or less antique kind of rug that has not been made for decades. Among these the expert and the amateur can choose according to their personal tastes.

A collection is based on other criteria. While for easily understandable reasons the amateur chooses in terms of the decoration of his home, the collector is guided first and foremost by his inclinations. He may be tempted to collect rare rugs from various regions or all the available types of a particular group. Competently conducted collecting not only occupies one's leisure time but also leads to experiment and many changes. Of course, the items in a collection are in part packed away in cases and occasionally alternated with those in use. Thus, a tastefully furnished house undergoes a kind of renovation. Besides, the monetary value of a collection gradually increases, provided the choice was good.

The purpose of a collection is to acquire, if possible below the asking price, only ancient, rare, particularly notable specimens in good condition, or examples that are important from the viewpoint of the history of the art. In order to become an expert, to be able to recognize quality rugs, one is advised to go regularly to museums in which rugs are displayed and to study good-quality illustrations in specialist publications. Constant testing of one's knowledge of the field is possible only if one observes the peculiarities of the rug at hand. In order to learn to determine which of a number of knotted rugs are valuable as real art objects, one must have experience, patience, and a certain healthy curiosity.

Most modern Oriental rugs consist of pieces intended for daily use and are variable in quality, lacking the artistic worth and originality of the older knotted rugs. It makes little difference whether they are produced in workshops or at home; they do not have the charm of the folk art that created the older rugs and they do not achieve the marvelous effects possible with vegetable dyes. Only rugs very finely knotted in certain manufactories mindful of their tradition, and in certain rural collectives, for example an Ispahan, a Kashan, or a Naïn rug, occasionally attain the heights of the old artistic artisanry by reason of their subtle designs. In modern production, only a few pieces of rural artisanry, or works of nomadic communities in remote regions, can be counted as collectors' items. Among the rugs made by nomads and peasants for their own use one still finds pieces that are worth the effort of collecting because of their originality in terms of folklore, vegetable dyes, and other qualities.

What kinds of Oriental rugs ought one to suggest to the future collector? This is primarily a question of personal preference, whether for rugs from a specific area or for special types, such as prayer rugs, but it also depends on one's financial ability. Collecting rugs of the classic period up to 1750 is almost out of the question because they are already in museums and their warehouses, or else in the great private collections. Besides, one would be most unlikely to acquire such items, even in a fragmentary state, at a reasonable price, because they are priced in the tens of thousands. On the other hand, one can hope to make sound purchases of well-preserved rugs of the period from 1750 to 1850 when old private collections are broken up and sold. It is also not uncommon to find rugs made after 1850 at art dealers', in good specialty shops, or at auctions, often at prices lower than those for pieces from private collections.

The collector encounters fascinating opportunities to specialize in some particular branch of the art. Of necessity, some limitation must be put on a collection. One possibility is to reconstruct completely given groups of rugs by collecting all the varieties still in existence, such as, for example, the ancient Qashqai (Shiraz) rugs, or the Bergamos. One could also limit one's collection to the varieties of a group produced at intervals of twenty to thirty years and thus concentrate on the problems of the development and decline of the periods in question.

It is interesting, too, to follow the spread and variations of specific patterns through rugs of various origins. There is an amazing and various multitude of older rugs from Turkey (Anatolia) and the Caucasus, dating from the time between 1850 and 1920. The same period produced a host of varieties among the rugs of the nomadic Iranian tribes—the Afshars, the Baluchis, the Kurds, the Luris, the Shasevanis, etc. The rugs made contemporaneously by the different Turkoman tribes of Central Asia are espe-cially instructive. Another point of departure might be to collect urban and village rugs, for instance, the Senneh and Feraghan rugs of Persia as well as the Hereke and Kumkapu rugs originating in Turkey. Most of the rugs made before the end of the nineteenth century may be regarded as worth collecting, since their wool was colored with vegetable dyes in most cases, but above all because the producers' individual artistic sense is clearly expressed in the designs. They afford the collector the possibility of studying the relations between style and the history of civilization. At the same time, he will take into consideration not only the rugs but the knotted work of lesser size, such as bedside mats, hangings, camel bags (*hurdi*), saddle blankets, and decorative bands (*khiva*), which contain almost all the original ornaments and symbols. These objects were usually made to fill personal needs and, consequently, decorated with traditional motifs. The successful amassing of a fairly wide collection of rugs presupposes a subject that has been carefully thought out. Choosing a direction for a collection compels one to stick to a single category and to search for true works of art. A collection will be judged not by the number of items in it but by their quality. Money is less important than competence and luck when one is buying. The collector spends enchanted days in search and anticipation until he becomes the happy owner of the piece he or she wants.

Another acceptable method of collecting consists of furnishing the rooms of one's home with rugs of the same style but of different varieties of a uniform group of rugs. A simpler though no less inviting solution, adapted by many amateurs, consists in choosing a characteristic rug from each of the areas important in the knotter's art (Turkey, the Caucasus, Iran, Central Asia, China, etc.).

5
Manufacturing Technique, Material, Labor

The technique of making Oriental rugs is virtually the same everywhere. There are, however, three different forms of production and methods of manufacture. Tribes of herdsmen, subject to the frequent moves imposed by their flocks' pasturage, and forced to interrupt their knotting labors frequently, generally can make only rugs of modest size. These nomads or seminomads use the most ancient device, placed horizontally on the ground, before which they crouch to weave and knot (see illustrations on pages 99 and 103). Settled peasants, on the other hand, almost always have vertical looms in their houses and are thus able to make larger rugs. In the urban manufactories, frames made of beams as long as trees are aligned side by side, and the knotters work at them under a supervisor and produce quite large rugs from sketched models.

In principle, the frame is the same in all cases: two side uprights and two traverses (beams or rollers). Two lighter wood separating bars—heddles—are added, on movable mountings and joined by ropes and knots that serve during the weaving operation to separate the alternate warp threads (compartmentation) and allow the woof threads (pick) to pass through. The side uprights are unnecessary on the nomads' horizontal weaving device, in which the two beams on which the warp threads move are fixed by pegs driven into the earth, the warp thus being kept under tension in its horizontal position.

The warp threads are first rolled around the traverses of the frame and stretched equally. Then a selvage is woven onto their lower ends to serve as a base for the knotting operation. Thus, the knotting threads become "knots" one after another horizontally on pairs of warp threads. After each row of finished knots, two or more woof threads are then woven. This is how the structure of the rug—composed of the warp, the knots, and the woof—is formed. Once the knotting is completed, the rug is finished off with a woven selvage. The side borders are then whipped with wool thread, and the warp threads (fringe) hanging at either end of the rug are trimmed, plaited, and knotted. Finally, the surface, from which irregular lengths of the knots still hang, is sheared smooth to form the pile, and then the rug is washed. Because of the preparation of the material (matching colors, preparing the warp, dyeing), and above all, because of the knotting of threads, row by row, by which the design is created, the manufacturing process as a whole is tedious and time-consuming. Three workers need about a year to make a finely knotted rug of average size.

The deeper the pile, the more the knotted rug reminds one of fur. When the knotting technique was invented, it was probably necessary to make "artificial furs" intended to protect against the chill of the ground. Knotting a rug meant enriching the weave with wool threads attached separately to the warp threads. Their "tufted" ends protruded from the surface and constituted the base of the rug, while their loops passing two by two around the warp threads made the knots visible on the smooth underside. The technique of the knotted rug is certainly based on normal weaving (warp and woof), but the knotted warp together with the knots that make up the body of the rug itself are its distinguishing characteristic. Tying is done with either the Turkish or the Persian knot, known in the Near East as the *turkibaff* and the *farsibaff*. Although they are called knots they have little in common with an ordinary knot. If the knotted threads were joined by whatever expedient means to the basic weave, the rugs would lose the chief advantage of their construction, their great elasticity. Properly speaking, the "knots" are supple stitches that retain the capacity of variable stretching even though they are firmly held in the closed "weave." The elastic property of the knots, moreover, is a unique function of the craftsman-like knotting of Oriental rugs. The Turkish knot is also called the "whole knot" because its loop completely encircles the pair of warp threads while its ends come out between them. The Persian knot, in contrast, encircles only one of the pair of warp threads, but its ends are better balanced because one comes out between each warp thread. That is why this is also called the "half-knot"; for no apparent reason it is also known as the "Senneh knot." (Senneh rugs are always made with Turkish knots.)

The chief materials used for Oriental rugs are sheep's wool, cotton, and less frequently, silk, all handspun. As a rule, a rug is made entirely of wool, though it may have a warp and woof of cotton. In addition to sheep's wool, camel's hair is also used occasionally for the knotting. Goat's hair is sometimes used, generally for the warp only. Silk may be used both for knots and the warp. From the technical point of view, the flexibility and elasticity of wool makes it the best and the most natural material for all the threads of the knotted rug. The fleece of Asian sheep is resistant and solid; one might almost say it had been made for Oriental rugs.

The different kinds of rugs show more or less marked structural characteristics. The following factors in the technical analysis of a rug's structural characteristics may provide clues as to its origin:

1. First, one must examine the material and

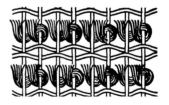

(Left) The Turkish or whole knot; (Right) the Persian or half-knot.

(Left) Schematic drawing of the knotting of the Turkish knot. (Right) Schematic drawing of the knotting of the Persian knot.

ascertain the number of strands or plies constituting the warp, woof, and knots of the rug in tight or loose twist, working from the left or from the right. The nature, thickness, and the way in which the threads are twisted play important parts in the workmanship. These give the rug its special properties as a whole.

2. The way in which the woof threads are inserted into the base weave chiefly determines the rug's structural character. It governs the positioning of the warp threads, the position of the knots, and the direction of the threads on the face of the rug. If two or more woof threads are treated in the usual weaving manner—in opposing waves—the warp threads will align themselves flat, the knots will be horizontal, and the back of the rug will be smooth. If, however, every second woof thread is kept straight and tight, every other warp thread will then be raised. This stratifies the base weave in two levels, in which, depending on the degree of tension in the woof threads, the even warp threads will be 30 to 90 degrees above the odd warp threads. The knots are then somewhat inclined, and in such case the back of the rug is ribbed. The upper threads, too, are more tightly compressed. This ribbing makes the structure of the rug stiffer.

3. The most important part, of course, is the face of the rug—which makes it fulfill its practical and artistic purposes. In most rugs the face has an individual quality in terms of the depth of the pile (in millimeters) and the texture (smooth or rough). Attention must also be given to the quality of the wool (fineness of the strands, elasticity, brilliance) as well as to its tightness (number of knots).

4. The way in which a rug is finished off is also important. Whether the ends of the rug are woven, and the tips of the warp threads are knotted or plaited, whether the rug ends simply in loose fringes, whether the sides have been edged with gathered lateral warp threads or have been woven flat—all these are characteristics peculiar to the different kinds of rugs.

5. The tightness of the knots can be determined by counting an area 10 centimeters square on the back of the rug. This figure, multiplied by 100, will give the number of knots to the square meter. The delicacy of the knotting is classified according to the following scale:

Very coarse: 4 to 8 knots per square centimeter —40,000 to 80,000 per square meter.

Coarse: 8 to 12 knots per square centimenter— 80,000 to 120,000 per square meter.

Average: 12 to 24 knots per square centimeter— 120,000 to 240,000 per square meter.

Fine: 24 to 36 knots per square centimeter— 240,000 to 360,000 per square meter.

Very fine: 36 to 50 knots per square centimeter —360,000 to 500,000 per square meter.

Extremely fine: 50 to 100 knots per square centimeter—500,000 to 1 million per square meter.

6
Patterns, Motifs, Kinships of Style

The ornamentation of Oriental rugs is based on ancient traditional rules having to do with the arrangement of spaces. Learning these rules will familiarize us with every kind of design. First, the rug is divided into field and borders. The field surface is also called the ground. Since all the design systems are based on their geometric arrangement of the field, it is possible to analyze the design forms with the help of a geometric diagram.

If the ground is divided into equal squares, one arrives at a kind of checkerboard. If each square is replaced by a repeated pattern, the result is a "design with simple alignment of motifs." But if every second square is replaced with a pattern of a different form, the result is an "alternating-motif design." If diagonals are drawn through the field to intersect at equal intervals, one obtains the well-known rhomboid division. A motif placed at the intersection of the rhombuses produces a "staggered-motif design." If still other ornaments, differing from those that have gone before, are put inside the diamonds, the result is a "staggered alternating-

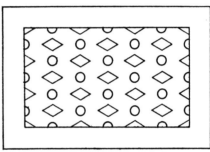

Staggered design—alternate forms

motif design." Such arrangements are also employed in various combinations. They differ in their proportions and are subject to infinite variations. That is why they are called "designs approaching infinity." Many keep the linear arrangement of the field, though often marked by straight spear-shaped leaves or tendrils in arabesques. Most often, however, the division gives way to pure design. The arrangement of the field in squares is sometimes converted to an alignment of octagons (as, for instance, in Afghan and Bokhara rugs). The diamonds are often replaced by hexagons, whence a "honeycomb design" with ornamental fillings.

The division of the field by parallel lines

21

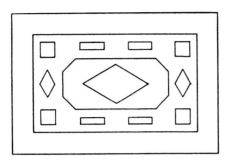

Grouped arrangement of design

Pointed oval medallion in rhomboid form

running diagonally or longitudinally, within which there are similar or varied motifs, is know as "diagonal" or "longitudinal" design (for instance, Baluchi, Kum, and Talish rugs). Some forms of design have tree, shrub, or flower motifs at one end of the field. This is called "ascending design." The category also includes the prayer rug with its niche pointing in one direction.

In contrast to these systems of running decoration, there are the central arrangements of motifs, in which a principal subject placed in the center is surrounded by subordinate smaller forms, arranged symmetrically and radially. This is known as "grouped-order design," coordinated by the longitudinal and horizontal axes of the field. The best-known form is the "medallion," which is typical of rugs of Persian make. Since it is invariably a much enlarged cross-section, it has also been used in a "row of medallions" to ornament rugs (for example, the Turkish Ushak rugs). The basic forms of the medallion are the rhombus, the rosette, and the star. The geometric designs of rugs by peasant artists always have the medallions—usually in rows of three in the middle of the field—in their original forms of rhombuses, hexagons, octagons, or star groups (for instance, Qashqai, Kazak, Shirvan, and Karabagh rugs). Persian and Turkish display rugs have oval-ended diamond

Round medallion

Eight-pointed star medallion

Concentric system of arabesques

22

Spiraled tendril

Stag

Forked arabesque or tendril

Heron

Lion attacking an ox

medallions artistically made of arabesques, medallions of circular rosettes, or medallions of sixteen-pointed stars. In addition, the corners of the field are filled with quarter-medallions of other shapes.

Ornaments imitated from nature are composed essentially of various scrolls and flower motifs. Lively spiral arabesques occupy the backgrounds of medallion rugs or are arranged in rows that wind around one another without a medallion. The intersections of undulant arabesques produce complex diamonds and play a large part in border decoration. The tendrils bear rosettes of flowers and numerous and varied palmettes, as well as buds and leaves. To this are added many shapes in interplay—flowered and leafy scrolls, trees, shrubs, bushes. But very frequently such designs also contain symmetrically arranged figures of animals—deer, gazelles, elk, rams, lions, leopards—as well as depictions of combat between animals or birds such as pheasants, geese, herons, etc., which often are also introduced into the medallions and the borders. More than one antique rug also depicts hunting scenes with horsemen and archers. Here and there, mythological figures appear.

Objects such as lamps, vases, pots, etc., are used in ornamentation. Moreover, various kinds of flowers—pinks, tulips, roses, hyacinths, etc.—

23

Rose motif   *Iris motif*   *Palmette calyx*

come into various rug designs. All these natural motifs are taken from more or less highly stylized forms—sometimes so highly stylized as to transform them beyond recognition and make them seem simply abstract decorations—characteristic abstract motifs, known as arabesques, and also the cloud bands and spheres, the cartouches, the well-known *mini-botah,* the pomegranate, the whorled calyx, and many others. As a result of the combination of motifs, standardized patterns of repetition have been developed—the famous *do-gule, mina-khani,* and Herati designs.

The geometric ornamentation of the rugs is composed either of motifs that follow one of the original linear arrangements of the field and form a reticulated base for regularly ordered full ornamentation, or of squares, lozenges, hexagons, octagons, and polygons of various sizes, arranged in groups. There are also small decorative elements, distributed regularly or scattered inside and around large forms. Through the most extreme stylization of plants, flowers, and figures, they represent an addition to the geometric ornaments; so, for instance, where there

are now latch-hook motifs, there were formerly tendrils, flowers, and plants, the shapes of which have been stylized into latch hooks. The polygonal motifs of the Turkoman rugs, in spite of their purely geometrical shape, retain their old names—*gul, gül, göl,* all included under *gülcha* ("flower, floweret"). Similarly, the many varied ornaments, sawtoothed and hooked, as well as the crab, scorpion, and wineglass motifs of the Caucasian rugs, are almost without exception plants, flowers, and leaves reduced to geometric forms. The polygons ranged in hooked tiers, various star groupings, and spoked medallions of the Caucasian region have their origin in floral forms, stylized wreaths, and bouquets of long-stemmed flowers. The scatterings of little figures of men and animals act as amulets.

Many kinds of rugs have single borders, but triple borders are generally preferred. They consist of one large main border flanked by narrow accompanying borders. To this is added a joined border also known as the hem. Among them slender stripes are inserted to make the separations. Especially luxurious rugs have as many as

24

Cartouche   Botah (mir) *motif*   *Herati design*

twelve to sixteen richly ornamented borders and stripes. Simple borders are most often occupied by a row of aligned or alternating motifs, while showpieces have borders of palmettes against a continuous movement of scrolls, rosettes, arabesque leaves, or various shapes of cloud bands and cartouches.

Kinships of style among the various kinds of rugs cannot be explained simply by tribal migrations or by merchants' comings and goings. The belief that there is a harmony in forms of design and in ornamentation, that there is a real similarity among widely separated periods and places, is based above all on the limited possibilities of the artistic form itself. Those who made the rugs could not go beyond the limits set by the art of textile working. In fact, the "revolutionary" concentric design of the Persian medallion rugs itself represents no more than an enlarged section projected on the whole surface of the field of a design conforming to the rug with alternating motifs. There are kinships of style as well between the medallion rugs and the motifs grouped in the center of the Egyptian Mameluke rugs and also, for instance, the early Ottoman rugs dating from the fifteenth century. The first Ushak rugs of Asia Minor also afford models of stylistic kinship with the Turkoman rugs of Central Asia. What is also striking is the close relationship between the designs and motifs of the Qashqai rugs of southern Persia and those of rugs from parts of the Caucasus, as well as the kinship between the Anatolian Bergamo and Yuruk rugs and some Kazak types. Analogous comparisons can be drawn among families of rugs with numerous similarly ornamented specimens since the eighteenth century, which have the *do-gule, mina-khani,* Herati, Feraghan, and Chichi designs. The total adoption of all the ornamentation of the Persian- and Ottoman-made rugs by the Spanish, Indian, and Turkish makers causes no surprise, for rugs of courtly art, like their makers, were exchanged internationally and sent long distances as gifts. More surprising are the similarities between a Khotan "box *gul*" type from the depths of eastern Turkestan and a Gendja from the Caucasus (see illustrations on pages 60 and 126).

7
Natural Colors, Aniline Colors, Effects of Color

Without the unique effect of its colors, the Oriental rug would have far less special beauty and artistic worth. The richness of its coloring is expressed not in the number of colors but above all in their quality and composition, often limited to the contrasting of four to eight colors. The sumptuous colors of Oriental rugs have long been a marvel. They stimulated Renaissance artists to a new treatment of painters' colors.

One has only to reflect on the primitive freshness or solemn sobriety of the major colors of peasant or nomad rugs, or on the harmonizing colors of rugs made in cities—most of the pieces offer the same visual quality as colors in nature. If one looks at them close up, they blend like the coloration of petals, insects' wings, or precious stones composed of flecks of light and dark tones, of varyingly accented stippling. Their great effect is founded on the play of tiny spots of different tones that makes the coloration "live." Out of the colored particles that vibrate before the eye and impel the retina to blend them is born a unit of living color that in its final effect makes the whole luminous, warm, and supple. Hence

the beautiful coloring of the Oriental rug results from the irregularity of its various colors. In addition, the sheen of the wool breaks up the light rays differently in each position, and this makes the colors change and shimmer. Thus is created a broad scale of graduated colors, the gentle contrast of which merges in the eye in an impression of full, splendid color, similar to the "color as light" of Impressionist painting. In the past these color effects resulted from a method of dyeing that was "insufficient in itself," done at home, and based on vegetable colors.

Due to the prolonged effect of light, air, humidity, and surface wear, the patina of age has further served to soften the colors. After aniline dyes were introduced, similar effects were achieved with these colors, which withstand light and washing. By resorting to soft half-tones, one can imitate the tone of rugs made with vegetable dyes. The new rugs are also treated chemically when they are finished, or they are exposed for some time to the sun in order to soften the intensity of their colors. In fact, the chemical industry's colors are much too "perfect" to be really beautiful. They impregnate the wool fibers so deeply and cover them so evenly that the colored surface becomes hard and lifeless. Aniline colors cannot achieve the wonderful effect of natural colors. That is why collectors and enthusiasts much prefer old-style rugs colored according to the ancient natural methods, or those new kinds that still have colors of essentially vegetable origin.

Even today the wool for the rugs of the nomadic tribes especially and for many rugs of provincial origin is colored wholly or partly with vegetable dyes. The reason is simple: It costs these normally poor people almost nothing but time and work to obtain such colors. Such plants as the madder, in particular, whose root is a source of red, grow wild in the Orient, or they can be cultivated, like the indigo plant, which produces blue. Hence the main colors of Oriental rugs are innumerable nuances of red and blue. The use of other vegetable materials and their special treatment, redyeing, mixing, as well as steeping—before or after the actual dyeing—in different products result in a whole series of various tones of well-known colors—yellow, green, turquoise, brown, violet, etc. Since it gives violet-blue tones, sumac is sometimes used for blue, as are other plants of the indigo family (*Indigofera*). Turquoise can also be made from the isperek, a kind of euphorbia that produces yellow, either mixed with a metallic salt or with indigo. Yellow is derived from the isperek, the skin of the pomegranate, and more rarely, from saffron, which is expensive. The most resistant yellows are achieved by repeated overlays of a rather light yellow made of a base of vine leaves and henna, safflower, or isperek. Buckthorn produces a solid orange. Green is obtained by mixing an indigo extract with green colorant, or by adding a yellow solution to vitriol, resulting in

beautiful dark tones of moss green, but wool does not take this treatment very well. Brown and its gradations toward rust or olive come from dwarf oak galls and acorns, mixed with madder and isperek. In the past a violet-red was obtained from the resinous secretions of the insect *Coccus lacca* on the bark of certain trees.

The dyeing procedure is the same as that used in the earliest times for making rugs with simple domestic equipment and necessarily gives uneven results. Plunged into the coloring solution in earthenware or copper vessels heated from below, the strands of wool absorb the color irregularly because of the unequal thicknesses of the handspun material, the fat content of the fibers, and finally, the air bubbles on their surfaces. The strands therefore are uneven in color, naturally more so in the thicker fibers and less so in the thinner. Many factors—the stage of maturity of the plant, the water, the mordant, the proper heating of the vessels, and the washing—affect the beauty and fastness of the natural color. With a relatively restricted arsenal of coloring matter, an almost unlimited number of tones is produced. The coloration of a rug gains in effect and beauty, however, if it is not composed of too many colors, especially of mixed tones. The natural brilliance of the wool endows the colors with a life of their own by making them shimmer in the light and often glow like precious stones. The irregularity of the colors and the often sudden change of tone, called *abrash*, are typical characteristics of the colors of Oriental rugs made by home workers.

There are great variations in the durability of rug colors. Many natural dyes fade with time, but there are others that remain unchanged until the threads are worn out. The most expensive coloring matter—saffron—fades most quickly, and the cheapest—madder—usually lasts the longest.

Natural indigo often has little resistance, while its chemical successor is quite durable. A small change in color, however, does enhance the beauty of rugs. Weakening of strong colors often modulates the tonality, which becomes subdued and faded. That is why a large plant for chemically washing Oriental rugs was opened in 1907 in London. This "English washing" is intended to rid the rug of raw tones. Many specimens of beautiful colors were at first victims of this process, which virtually drained them of color. The deepest and most beautiful natural colors are to be found in the antique rugs of the Caucasus region and Turkestan. Most of those from Iran and Turkey have for decades been made only with aniline colors, while the tribes in general still use colors of their own composition. Aside from chemical analysis, one must have a keen eye and a great deal of experience to recognize natural colors.

Kashan. *The dyer of the skeins of wool is generally an independent artisan. He works to order and delivers the merchandise in the desired colors when he does not sell it in the bazaar. This merchant is carrying nine different colors—madder red, pink, dark, medium, and light blue, light green, yellow, brown, and olive—enough to make a variegated rug.*

After the newly sheared wool has been washed in water containing a good proportion of lime to remove the oil and other impurities, it is combed, sorted, and spun by hand. Then the threads are put into skeins for the dyeing and plunged for a certain amount of time in the hot caldron containing the dye.

Vegetable dyeing (madder, indigo, henna, etc.) is a laborious process. Obtaining the dyestuff and then doing the actual dyeing demands, in fact, a great deal of time and labor. In the rather important centers of rug production, aniline dyes produced by the chemical industry are preferred because they are simple and easy to use. The rural population, however, rather frequently still uses vegetable dyes.

8
Authenticity, Age, Value, Buying

When we say "a genuine rug," we obviously mean that there is a distinction to be drawn between handmade and machine-made rugs; at the same time we do not clearly indicate that we refer only to the Oriental rug. Since it has been known so long and so widely, it is strange that the Oriental rug has never been viewed in the right sense when it comes to the essence of this work of art. As far as technique is concerned, for centuries almost all the countries of Europe and North Africa have been making handknotted rugs in the effort to imitate the ornamentation and color of the Oriental rug. Even if well-known knotted rugs dating back as far as the fifteenth and sixteenth centuries and coming from Spain, Portugal, England, and later, Germany, Poland, Sweden, and the Balkans do represent more or less valuable copies and imitations of the Oriental rug, they are nonetheless pallid reproductions, like machine-made rugs, and their relation to the originals is like that of photography to painting. Even though they involved the same techniques, they still lack artistic content, and they are as devoid of the original essence as of the characteristics and

kinds of workmanship of genuine Oriental rugs. In them we do not feel the personal touch of the Oriental rug knotters in conceiving the rug as a whole or in arranging its forms and colors. Their simple equipment and their manual labor cause certain irregularities in the ground, structure, design, and especially colors. These are the natural concomitants of the Oriental rug and emphasize that an artistic conception and not a mechanical activity directs the hands. Those who see mistakes in them would prefer the imitation, or even a machine-made copy, to the original. (Which is not to say that obtrusive creases, distortions, holes, rips, and other real defects add to the rug.) If one supposed that various irregularities alone afford the most reliable clues to authenticity, one might overlook some of the finest pieces, in which the signs of hand workmanship do not force themselves on one's attention. There are many Oriental rugs that are properly and regularly knotted, especially among the older ones, but also in the current varieties from almost every area where they are made.

With some practice one can soon tell from

Rug merchant in the Kashan bazaar. *The rugs produced in central Persia are bought by wholesale merchants of the bazaars in Teheran, Kashan, Hamadan, etc., and then directed toward Western importing firms.*

the typical structure and from the finishing touches on ends and sides (see Chapter 5), but even more from the noble, original ornamentation and color (see Chapters 6 and 7), whether one is dealing with a genuine Oriental rug. If one has no experience, one can at least check the knots in this way: Fold the rug horizontally, press, and separate the threads. If there are aligned knots attached to the warp threads in the woven base, then one is really dealing with a knotted rug. In a machine-made rug, on the other hand, the threads seem to come out of the woven base. They do not coil around the warp threads but are simply attached in a U shape under the woven threads. From the dual viewpoints of wear and scope of artistic creation, there is an immeasurable difference between the two methods.

Even a copy made in the Orient itself can only rarely be exact because of the natural variations in handwork and therefore always becomes a work in its own right. Nevertheless, we do encounter certain categories of Oriental rugs that are imitations, intentional or unwitting. There are also, with due allowance for some forgeries executed by special processes, "authenticated" copies of sumptuous specimens dating from the high period of the art of knotted rugs. Pieces originating in Tabriz, Kashan, Kirman, and Sultanabad (now called Arak), as well as those produced in the Turkish manufactories of Hereke, Kumkapu, Panderma, etc., toward the turn of the century, belong to another category. Their makers sought to give life to the style and ornamentations of the classic rugs by resorting to appropriately fine knots. Thus, they produced works of a certain value, which are sought by collectors today. All these copies and imitations, even the counterfeits, are real knotted rugs. They are fakes only if their origin and age were

disguised at times of sale. Moreover, their value is still much higher than that of modern rugs. A third category includes those kinds of rugs in which design, colors, material, and technique are essentially unchanged from those of past generations. This preservation of tradition does not mean that such rugs, whether made by nomads or by village communities and urban manufactories, are copies or imitations in the sense of passing off a fraud.

Aside from collectors, in general only enthusiasts are interested in Oriental rugs—persons who choose to furnish their homes in period styles both of furniture and decoration. It is common knowledge that really old Oriental rugs in good condition are valued much more highly —and rightly so—than those of recent origin. Since the turn of the century this fact has led many Oriental firms and European merchants to find various ways of "aging" new rugs made with aniline dyes. In the Orient, the least damaging of these procedures was and still is to hang out the rug in a street in which traffic, dust, and sunlight will soon fade it. This was followed by the "washing" in European establishments described above. Today, unscrupulous merchants have the effrontery to describe perfectly new rugs as old even while pretending astonishment that the buyer wants something in as good shape as if it were new.

If in many cases the origin of less well-known rugs is not easy to establish, in most cases a more or less accurate determination of the age of antique knotted rugs presents almost insurmountable difficulties. One can fall back only on the practice and experience gained by meticulously applying stable values established through the scientific study of originals in museums and collections. One must seize every opportunity to compare rugs in order to perfect one's capacity to determine the type, origin, and age of a rug. But if one attaches no importance to developing one's own judgment, then it will be in one's interest when one is ready to buy a valuable rug to ask the help of a known expert or to consult a trustworthy firm of specialists.

The best indications in determining age are not merely ornamentation and color. Attention should also be paid to certain pecularities of structure and to the condition of the fabric, as well as to the weave as a whole. Compare the decoration, especially of the borders, with that of old examples in museums, and then the structure, the knot, the fabric of the warp and woof, as well as the finish of selvages, ends, etc., to see whether they correspond to those that usually characterize a rug of given origin. Colors can be compared only with those of originals.

Age, state of preservation, and rarity play special parts in the appraisal of Oriental rugs. The rugs should then be examined for fineness of knot, quality, and beauty. Apart from rugs of the great classic period, the value of which is virtually inestimable today, there are pre-1800 knotted pieces—though, to be honest, very few— that still come into the art market or onto the auction block.

Pieces that are important from the point of view of the history of the art command vast prices. Knotted rugs made before 1875 are valuable because of age. There are still many of them in private ownership as well as on the specialist market. Experts and enthusiasts value these pieces because they are unquestionably colored with vegetable dyes. Antique rugs, usually more than a hundred years old, command great attention because of their careful knotting and the intricate craftsmanship of their designs, while any special value is fully recognized. To be worth their prices, however, they ought to have pile of regular height, an undamaged base weave, and well-preserved borders. Very short pile is often quite as natural in these pieces as very fine structure. Until about 1910, in many parts of the Orient, thin rugs were regarded as being among the best and most sophisticated. Since in general they had fine, dense knots, they had to be sheared very close in order to bring out clearly the delicacy of the design. Antique rugs are made almost wholly of quality materials—which is the main reason they have lasted so long. Valuation of antique rugs is based first of all on the fineness of the knot. More coarsely knotted pieces, however, can exceed finely knotted ones in value if they are older, rarer, or more beautiful. On the basis of the criteria discussed, such specimens can be worth $400 to $1,000 a square meter.

Each period of knotting has its own traits. Although hard for the unskilled eye to recognize, they appear in the structure, color, and changes in ornamentation and material used for the different kinds of rugs. A generally known instance of decline in value coincided with the introduction of aniline dyes in certain areas of production. That is why we classify a large number of the Oriental rugs made between 1875 and 1935 as old but not necessarily valuable. There are many exceptions, however, among these varieties of rugs originating in the "aniline period" that have little or no chemical coloration. Their value lies chiefly in their still meticulous workmanship. If these rugs do not use yarns dyed with industrial products that were bad at the time, if they are still in good condition, they are valued—depending on their delicacy, rarity, and quality—at three or four times more than corresponding new examples of the same kinds.

Even new rugs made since World War II present very diverse peculiarities of structure, color, design, and degrees of quality. Aesthetically and qualitatively, they may differ widely in value. It is relatively simple to appraise them, however, because in the export and domestic trade they are priced as "by-the-yard" merchandise. If one wants to buy a new rug that will hold up well, one that is priced below $60 the square meter will seldom fill the need. But one can be sure of quality, beauty, and good workmanship in rugs priced from $60 to $100 per square meter. Those of better quality, in view of the time and cost of production, can be worth from $200 to $600 the square meter for a knot density of 360,000 to 500,000. High prices are not necessarily a guarantee of actual value and quality. In such cases it is advisable to call in the services of an expert before buying. Nor should the finest knotting be allowed to deceive one as to possible poor quality of the wool. Very finely knotted pieces are certainly the costliest, but the true value does not always depend on the fineness of knotting. Many trashy rugs have a staggering density of knots, especially figured rugs.

If one wants to buy an Oriental rug, one goes to a reliable specialist firm that accepts responsibility for the merchandise it sells. Even in the most expensive places, one can often make better buys than from those alluring places set up only on a fly-by-night basis. In order to be certain whether a rug will blend well with one's surroundings, one should preferably observe it in the spot where it will be used. The first characteristic of quality is even structure and flexibility combined with toughness without any concern for knot density. In case of doubt, beauty of design and harmony of color can be given preference. If the rug is too stiff or too limp to the touch, it will not wear well. Rugs valuable for their rarity or their age are, of course, exceptions.

Tears, holes, and raveled selvages and ends are not "signs of age," even in old specimens. The best way of detecting possible flaws is to study the underside of the rug. Folds are almost inevitable in the nomads' rugs, but if they are not noticeable, take away none of the value. Somewhat "light" areas are unacceptable except in specimens of very rare age. Similarly, it is only in antique rugs that slightly washed-out colors are not considered to reduce the value. Many new rugs have wool of exceptional brilliance. This is often achieved by a "shine wash" done in Europe, but its effect does not last long.

9
Use and Care of
the Oriental Rug

During his hectic day every man longs to be at home among his own things to relax and reflect. Such an atmosphere is created by beautiful furniture and artistic Oriental rugs. Whether a residence is designed in the modern, spacious style or arranged in a more traditional mode, there is hardly any room decor that is not enhanced by an Oriental rug. Rugs of geometric pattern fit well into modern rooms; various medallion rugs or other fine designs of flowers and tracery harmonize with period furniture. A rug can augment or reduce the feeling of space. It can enliven or calm an atmosphere, make it formal or friendly, intimate or elegant. That is why each rug should be chosen judiciously in terms of size, color, and ornamentation. It should also be suitable to the room's purpose. A light rug makes a room seem larger, a dark one makes it seem smaller, and one with luminous colors increases the light. Rectangular rugs or runners can extend space optically, two different rugs placed transversely shorten or subdivide it, and a rug placed somewhat on the bias changes its perspective. A rectangular throw placed in a passage

joins two spaces. The medallion rug is best left unoccupied; at most it will take an ornamental table and chairs. Nor should it be forgotten that rugs ought not only to match the style but also to suit the arrangement from the functional point of view. Valuable old rugs or thin, delicate ones are out of place in a heavily used room, in corridors, at doors, or under the dining table. But there are many kinds of sturdy Oriental rugs that are better suited to such rough use because of their thick wool and special resilient qualities. Rugs with a repeated design become boring in a large area, but they can set one another off when they are varied. That is why it is best, before one buys a rug, to live with it for a while in the place where it will be used. For hangings, one should choose only rugs knotted as lightly and thinly as possible, with designs that seem to "climb"—that is, ornamentation that is ascendant only—or with one of the prayer rug's stylized forms of architectural niche in its central field.

A reasonable "middle way" is recommended for the care of Oriental rugs, which are particularly resistant to wear because their elasticity

gives them a natural capacity for endurance. The wool used, too, is generally of a sturdy kind, with strong threads. It is easily cleaned, for a quality wool throws off dirt. Nevertheless, one must not suppose that these "works of art thrown underfoot" have unlimited resistance to wear. Careless cleaning with chemical products or modern devices (vacuum cleaners with beating attachments) is harmful to them. The movement of furniture back and forth and the uncontrollable friction of rubber soles affect their longevity. It is quite sufficient to use an ordinary vacuum cleaner on them once a week. For major cleaning, wipe the surface with a damp cloth and then vacuum the underside. Dust and spills can also be got rid of with a damp cloth. A little turpentine added to the water keeps away moths and revives colors. In winter, rugs should be put out for several hours in dry snow wherever this is possible. Spots must be removed at once, both sides of the rug being sponged with plenty of liquid before one attacks the interior of the weave. During the summer, rugs should be sprayed two or three times with antimoth treatment, never to be cleaned chemically unless it is heavily soiled in its base weave.

Washing rugs in Iran. *The finished rugs are carefully sheared, brushed, and finally washed. South of Teheran, close by ancient Rhages (called Rai today), rises the source of the Sheshma-Ali River. For centuries during the hot season the people of the vicinity have washed their rugs here and then spread them out in the sun to dry.*

10
Turkish Rugs

Between the ninth and the thirteenth centuries, during the development of the Turkish Seljuk states, the weaving of knotted fabrics became widespread. It reached its first peak during the thirteenth century in the Anatolian kingdom of the Rum Seljuks. The richly varied ornamentation of the eighteen great Seljuk rugs found in the great mosque of Konia (Rum, formerly Iconium) and Beshir consists of variously stylized vegetable shapes and geometric motifs that, in their flowing alignment, resemble ingenious latticework. There are designs of staggered octagons that recall *gul* motifs similar to the flowers of the Turkoman rugs. There are also squares filled with stars, hooked ornaments arranged diagonally, palmettes with stems, as well as rhomboid and hexagonal forms filled with flowers and bordered with leaves. Lines that turn back on themselves at a right angle link the major motifs. Borders are garnished with large hooked shapes. The first known prayer rug with niches also belongs to the Konia discoveries. Its colors are strict and sober. They are composed of two shades of red, as well as blue, green, some yellow, brown, and white. The Seljuk rugs are wool, both warp and woof, with 160,000 Turkish knots to the square meter. If these pieces, now on display in the Islamic Art Museum in Istanbul, have withstood more than a half-millennium of wear, it is because, being mosque rugs, they were walked on only by bare feet.

After the Mongol whirlwind carried away the Seljuk Empire, the tribe of Osman or Othman took power in Anatolia about 1300. The early Ottoman period of rugmaking began with the production of three standard models, the ornamentation of which consisted thereafter of alternate geometric forms in combination with vegetable elements.

The first major type has a blue background on which rows of light octagons with emphasized outlines are staggered with diamonds composed of red leaf patterns in arabesques. The decoration of the borders is a kind of braiding developed from Kufic script. In the second major type the octagons and the diamonds alike are formed into a grillework of leaves in arabesques and half-palmettes. Done in bright yellow, they stand out splendidly from the warm red background. Palmettes, rosettes, cloud bands in the shape of

Ghiordes silk prayer rug (Ghiordes-Namaslik). *Turkey, nineteenth century, 165 by 118 centimeters. Warp: silk. Woof: cotton. Pile: silk, 5 millimeters long. Density of knotting: 234,000 Turkish knots per square meter. Structure: thin, glossy, pliable. Prayer rugs constitute one of the most diverse categories of knotted rugs. Ghiordes rugs are one of the classic types. The relatively small niche (mihrab), generally resembling a Gothic window with two columns, is characteristic. A lamp or ewer (ibrik) hangs in the pediment, and above it are two floral arabesques and a decorative panel. Richly ornamented borders surround the niche.*

Ladik prayer rug (Ladik-Namaslik). *Turkey, early twentieth century, 143 by 95 centimeters. Warp and woof: wool. Pile: wool, 8 milli-meters. Density of knotting: 104,000 Turkish knots per square meter. Structure: thick, full, pliable. Unlike the classic Ladik, this new type has only a simple niche and the forms of abstract flowers in place of tulips in the decorative panels. The light and dark stripes of the middle borders (sobokli, or "pipe stems") are the determining characteristics of the Kula prayer rug.*

the Greek letter omega, and cartouches in the border already foreshadow the Ushak rugs. The design system and motifs of both types are still closely related to those of the Turkoman rugs. The second type is known as the "Holbein rug," although it shows no sign of any influence by Holbein's paintings, but rather, recalls those of Lorenzo Lotto (1480–1556). A major motif characterizes the third type. This is a large square in which an octagon is contained, and it is repeated three times in the length of the field. Side by side with this coordinated alignment of ornaments, small rugs were already being made with a single main motif and subordinate groupings of accompanying motifs. The borders have rows of rosettes. The blue-and-yellow coloring of this type shows violent contrasts. Variations of the first two kinds were produced only until the thirteenth century, while the style of the third type survived until very recently in the Bergamo rugs.

Classic kinds of Turkish rugs appeared concurrently in Egypt, where they were made from 1260 on in the Mameluke sultans' court manufactory in Cairo, then after 1517 in the large works of the Osmanlis, who had conquered the city. For a long time the Mamelukes continued making rugs of purely Turkoman character. As the rug fragments from the Mameluke tombs at Fostat (Old Cairo) show, the Turkomans introduced the art into Egypt. In the beginning these were Turkomans in the service of the Edzhub dynasty (Turkish-Egyptian militia), which took power under tht name of Mamelukes. Other Turkish tribes (the Chokas, for instance) reached Moorish Spain at the same time by way of North Africa. There, too, rug production began. The specimens remaining from the fifteenth century still show Turkoman design influence.

The ornamentation of the Mameluke rugs (Damascus rugs) has its stylistic base in the Turkoman rugs, but it was developed under the influence of Coptic textile art. The marvelous example in the Austrian Museum of Applied Arts, with knots of silk, gives some idea of these rugs and of their principle, which consists of kaleidoscopically grouping motifs with a single design each. The central motif, placed on a background in the form of a star, appears as a medallion composed of large octagons one within another. Around this motif are grouped geometric forms that occupy the whole of the field. This grouping is repeated three times in the length of the rug. Small Mameluke rugs have only one central motif with accompanying forms, and in the corners of the field, octagons of medium size. The arrangement of the motif gives them a resemblance to the medallion rugs that surely inspired the authors of the Persian designs. Delicate and naturalistic ornamental leaves, linked by slender tendrils and placed close together, fill the geometric ornaments, the intermediate fields, and the borders. Alongside the luminous tones of red and blue, a warm yellow and a green are the dominant colors. Shape and color penetrate each other in such a way that no part of the surface is left untouched. The Mameluke rugs are knotted entirely of wool, with 150,000 Persian knots to the square meter (300,000 when in silk). The height of their development occurred in the fifteenth and sixteenth centuries, and the composition and color of these rugs are unique in the history of the art.

The classical period of Ottoman rugmaking was launched at the start of the sixteenth century with the extension of Turkish domination to parts of three continents. Centers developed in rapid succession, fertilizing one another, and new stylistic tendencies appeared. The Ottoman style remained restricted to Asia Minor and Egypt. The Ottoman rug that Europeans called "Cairene" already enjoyed a worldwide reputation in the sixteenth century. It must therefore have been developed as early as the fifteenth century in the royal manufactory of Bursa, the Ottoman sultans' first residence in Anatolia. Here there was a huge production of rugs, some of which were shipped to Cairo. Ottoman-Cairene rugs were especially appreciated in Europe until the end of the eighteenth century, undoubtedly because of their baroque design, which perfectly suited the taste of the time. The number of design varieties was very large, and research has brought only some of them to light. The "Cairene" has a floral ornamentation composed essentially of notched, spear-shaped leaves, feathered and rolled, as well as palmettes, rosettes, and S-shaped arabesques. The construction of the design is based on a rhomboid system. Sometimes the diamond is used complete and becomes the major design, composed of straight, spear-shaped leaves. Two standard types of variant appear. In the first the major motif is composed of four palmettes framed by arabesques of matched leaves. This ornament is joined by S-shaped arabesques and garnished with spear-shaped leaves in staggered arrangement. Rosettes mark the corners of the divisions into diamonds. In the second type the major motif is composed of a large rosette with eight palmettes arranged in spoke fashion. It is distributed through the field at rather large regular intervals, and the S-shaped arabesques are used to fill the background. Many forms of design are also round medallions, filled with tulips and pinks in spoke arrangements, that are set staggered in the model or arranged evenly on the field (row of medallions). There are small rugs that have only a central medallion, whose quar-

ters also occupy the corners of the field. The borders have spear-shaped leaves flanked by palmettes and rosettes that often alternate with stemmed tulips and pinks. A warm red for the background, a yellowish green, a light blue, and much golden yellow produce the impressive coloring of the whole. The rugs are predominantly of pure wool or of wool and fine goat hair. Later, cotton and silk were used for warp and woof. The number of Persian knots is in the neighborhood of 200,000 per square meter, but sometimes it is as high as 700,000. Prayer rugs of this kind dating from the sixteenth century are perfect works of art. With their baroque niches and the richness of their ornamentation in the style of the Ottoman rugs, in fact, they are quite the most beautiful of all prayer rugs.

Other kinds of classic Ottoman rugs came into being at the same period in Turkey. They were developed in Ushak, in western Anatolia. Their style is distinguished from that of the early Ottoman types with geometric designs by an ornamentation that consists of rows of staggered medallions with arabesques and plants copied from nature, but they are closely related from the technical point of view. Many portrayals of them in paintings, well-preserved specimens going back as far as 1584, and heraldic emblems show that the Ushak makers received steady orders from Europe. Two principal groups were especially popular. One has round and oval medallions emphasized by wreaths of leaves and filled with arabesques and half-palmettes. Narrow rugs have a single row of round red medallions on a dark-blue background in staggered alternation with light-blue oval medallions divided into two by borders. The field is covered with greenish-yellow tendrils. The "medallion Ushak," as this type is called, is also found in broad shapes with two or three full rows of medallions, as well as

Melas prayer rug (Melas-Namaslik). *Turkey, beginning of the nineteenth century, 160 by 110 centimeters. Warp and woof: wool. Pile: wool, 6 millimeters long. Density of knotting: 165,000 Turkish knots per square meter. Structure: light, pliable, fine-grained. The Melas rugs of this period generally have, in the broad border and above the niche, palmettes and fairly naturalistic rosettes as well as arabesques that appear to be based on plant forms, while more recent examples have geometric ornaments. A small, narrow niche bordered by flowerets and with a crenellated gable, as well as the yellow-red coloring, characterizes the Melas. The prayer rug permits the pious Muslim to have an appropriate place for his devotions. The symbol of the niche (mihrab), which in every mosque points in the direction of the holy city of Mecca, reproduced on the rug serves the same end and transforms the place of prayer, wherever it may be, into a temporary sanctuary.*

Makri rug. *(Current name: Fethije). Turkey, twentieth century, 194 by 118 centimeters. Warp and woof: wool. Pile: wool, 8 millimeters. Density of knotting: 102,000 Turkish knots per square meter. Structure: full and slightly ribbed. Paired niches with opposed gables are characteristic of Makri rugs. In this example, two smaller niches, with stepped gables and medallions, are worked into the design. This type is called a "paired prayer rug."*

in small rugs with a single central medallion. The other type is known as the "star Ushak." On a red background this type has medallions in the form of eight-pointed stars made of arabesques, in staggered alternation with smaller diamonds made of arabesques. They are blue and green, with light decorative work. Tendrils or arabesques fill the background. Other Ushaks combine the ornamentation of the major types—wavy borders alternate with palmettes, with cloud bands in the omega shape.

The Ushak types with a white background constitute a separate group. The best-known type has rosettes of flowers in staggered alignment, each with four angular leaves that recall a stylized bird. Another has a motif of three little balls on two highly stylized leaves of cherry blossoms—whence their name, "ball rugs." The varicolored ornaments of these related designs stand out fresh and pleasant against the gray-white background. With the other types included in the group, the white-background prayer rugs in particular enjoy a prominent place. Their baroque niches and arabesque leaves give them a characteristic style.

It is not possible to list here the individual types of Ottoman rugs, but three variants ought to be mentioned. Prayer rugs with a number of niches in a row for communal meditation were specially made in Ushak for mosques. They are distinguished by the subtle ornamentation of the field and borders, with a wealth of delicately designed tendrils, arabesques, and palmettes. Another important variety is the "palmette Ushak" of the seventeenth century, with its arrangement of alternating palmettes. A variant of the type still made throughout the nineteenth century, the "Japrak Ushak," as its name indicates (*japrak* means "leaf"), is entirely decorated with stylized palmettes that resemble leaves. All the old Ushak rugs are knotted to a base fabric of wool. They have a short pile and consist of about 150,000 Turkish knots to the square meter. The later Ushaks, from the nineteenth century, however, were made with a deeper pile (8 to 10 millimeters) to meet Western requests.

Anatolian prayer rugs reached an exceptional peak as classic types in the seventeenth century. The oldest known example is the Seljuk prayer rug mentioned earlier, which goes back to the thirteenth century. The most beautiful specimens, already completely developed in terms of style, appeared in the Ottoman production of the sixteenth century. Since then, prayer rugs have constituted the most richly diverse of all knotted rugs. All stylistic tendencies appear in them, from simple geometric forms to subtle ornamentation, in accordance with the way in which the character of a people expressed itself in these religious objects. No one knows when it

 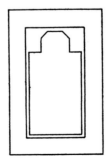 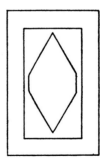

(Left) Schematic pattern of a prayer rug: plain gable; (Right) Schematic pattern of a prayer rug: horseshoe gable.

(Left) Schematic pattern of a prayer rug: geometric form of gable; (Right) Schematic pattern of a prayer rug: opposed niches.

became the custom to cover an unclean surface with a rug for the purpose of prayer. In any event, rugs were used very early for religious purposes. When the pious Muslim prays, wherever he is, he falls to his knees and touches his forehead and the palms of his hands to the ground. With his prayer rug (*namaslik,* in Turkish, he not only assures himself of a clean surface but at the same time transforms it into a temporary shrine, thanks to the symbol of the prayer niche (*mihrab*), which in every mosque points to the holy city of Mecca, and which serves the same purpose when it is reproduced on the rug. Even before Islam, the niche was a religious symbol because it served to frame the tree of life that was in the beginning the sign of rebirth. The niche with the tree of life is found on tombs in Central Asia, as well as on the Seljuks' stone coffins. After the conversion of the Turks, Islam absorbed this symbol into its own religious imagery.

The Muslim peoples of Persia, India, Turkestan, and the Caucasus, of course, also produced many prayer rugs with individual characteristics. But the richest choice and the great majority of types come mainly from the art of the Turkish Sunnite tribes, and from the various countries of Asia Minor in particular. The nomadic tribes and the peasants made their own prayer rugs, while town residents relied on the product of commercial makers. There are portable prayer rugs (*namaslik*) and larger ones for home use (*sedchade*), as well as rugs with numerous niches (*saph*) that are used for communal prayer. The characteristic of the prayer rug is not only the simple niche motif but also, frequently, two kinds of niche used in contrast in the field of the rug. The niche is often merely suggested by a single-direction construction of the geometric or floral ornamentation.

Ghiordes prayer rugs originated in the city of that name in western Anatolia. In earliest antiquity it was a source of medallion rugs and of others of mosaic design with octagons of great style and motifs and borders flowered with pinks and hyacinths. But the classic style of the prayer rug is particularly significant. It gained such renown that in the Orient the name of Ghiordes was the generic synonym for the Turkish knot. The Ghiordes type is almost square, and its niche is small and compact in comparison with the richness of the borders. The red, light-blue, or green niche resembles a Gothic window, occasionally bordered with flowers. It may also be divided by decorative verticals resembling columns. From its apex hangs a ewer (*ibrik*) or a lamp, most often composed of flowers. It is characterized by flowered traceries dominating the niche, as well as transverse lines with arabesque and cloud-band motifs. The ornamentation of the borders is composed of palmettes and leaves, or groups of four stylized pinks. With a base fabric of wool the Ghiordes is thin and light. It has a short, smooth pile like velvet and 160,000 to 300,000 Turkish knots to the square meter. In general, the colors are vivid but partly faded. In the manufactories of Panderma, Bursa, Kumkapu, etc., Ghiordes types were often made of silk. Thay have very precise ornamentation, with singular configurations in the borders, which is only rarely the case in homemade specimens. Among the special types we should mention the Kis-Ghiordes, with its facing niches and its small size, as well as the Basra-Ghiordes (see illustration on page 39).

Demirci prayer rugs are made in the city of that name near Ghiordes. Gaily colored and tightly knotted, they are products of family artisanry, very close in their ornamentation to the style of the Ghiordes and the Kula. The red or blue niche most often has a stepped gable edged with pothooks. There are about 120,000 Turkish knots to the square meter.

The Kula prayer rug, from that city and its region, also belongs to the classic group. It is long and has a large red or dark-blue niche. A flowered garland often hangs from the triangular gable. The main border, striped with narrow white and black longitudinal lines with minuscule flowers, such as appears also in the Ghiordes, is a frequent characteristic of Kula rugs. Otherwise the border has grouped, stylized floral motifs. The pile is short and smooth as velvet. A second type is the Masarli-Kula, or "cemetery rug." Its blue niche has horizontal divisions in which little narrow and broad trees (cypresses and pines), as well as little houses, alternate. The tree motif of this variety reminds us of cemeteries in Southern Europe, as does its color, which blends dark blue, ocher, fawn red, and light green. The Kula types have a base fabric of wool and a smooth nap of medium length; they average 160,000 Turkish knots to the square meter.

The Ladik prayer rug, again named for a town and its district, is the third classic type.

The antique Ladik is narrow. Its field is arranged in three divisions. The red niche, usually with three crenels or battlements, is generally placed low on the rug. The light-blue middle section is covered with leaves in yellow arabesques. The upper part, again with a red background, is characterized by a number of crenels with a row of tulips, an essential feature of this type. The wavy geometric arabesque in the wide border forms cartouches filled with colored flowers. The pile is of medium length. There are 200,000 Turkish knots to the square meter. Another type is the "column Ladik," so called because of the delicate columns that divide its *mihrab* into a middle niche and two smaller side ones. The gables are dominated by arabesques. In the horizontal bands there are rows of battlements with tulips. The delicacy of light coloring composed of blue, red, and yellow gives this prayer rug a legendary quality. The main border is again filled with oval cartouches of much color. In some variants the niche is replaced with a mosaic design of stylized flowers and leaves. The structure is delicate, but there are still about 240,000 knots to the square meter. New Ladik prayer rugs are almost square, with a long nap and

Mudjur multiple prayer rug (Mudjur-Saph). *Turkey, nineteenth century, 370 by 78 centimeters. Warp and woof: wool. Pile: wool, 7 millimeters long. Density of knotting: 122,000 Turkish knots per square meter. Structure: full, compact, pliable. The Mudjur prayer rug is characterized by the niche bordered with flowers, a stepped gable, generally with four steps, which bears an angled element with double latch hooks, as well as by small, repeated niches in the end borders, as in Turkoman rugs. Originally, the prayer rug was designed for meditation in company in the mosques. Some antique examples have a number of niches arranged in two or more rows.*

rather coarse knotting. They have a simple red niche and a border of simple geometric forms (see illustration on page 40).

The Bursa prayer rug is usually of silk, very finely knotted and especially thin. It has a baroque niche and a horseshoe arch and a delicate decoration in bright colors. But Bursa also produces wool rugs of great beauty, small and thin. The ornamentation consists of arabesques with especially elaborated flowered traceries. Since the turn of the century, Bursa has been making its prayer rugs with an eye to the export market, and the design is quite monotonous. All the old specimens have 300,000 knots or more (the new ones 140,000) to the square meter.

Melas prayer rugs are among the finest and most beautiful. The niche and borders in the old pieces have almost naturalistic floral ornaments, whereas the ornamentation of the later ones is usually geometric. The Melas can be recognized by its relatively small, light-red niches and its sharply crenellated gable. The wide borders have an arrangement of leafy tendrils with rosettes or stylized flowers in groups of four. The luminosity of the colors, with much yellow, the red of the *mihrab,* and the light blue of the borders, produces a particularly successful harmony of tones. The shape is almost square. But there are also very long, narrow Melas rugs, in which the field has two opposed niches framing a medallion with grouped motifs in the style of the "Transylvanian rugs." The pile is smooth and rather short. Some 150,000 Turkish knots to the square meter on a wool fabric result in a rather thin structure (see illustration on page 43).

Makri prayer rugs are made by the peasant population of that area, southeast of Smyrna. They are similar to the Melas in their coloring, but they have either two elongated niches side by side with different interiors, or niches with

gables pointing in opposite directions and arranged in pairs, which remind one of two boats side by side. Smaller, opposed niches, as well as a medallion, occupy the interior. All the components have violently contrasting colors in tones of light blue, orange, red, and white. The border, with its yellow background, is ornamented with geometric arabesques made of leaves and flowers. The full, deep pile has some 120,000 Turkish knots to the square meter (see illustration on page 44).

Mudjur prayer rugs, which come from this central Anatolian city and its region, are simple. The niche has a hooked, crenellated motif on its stepped gable. Occasionally it encloses a cruet (*ibrik*). Often the outline of the niche is emphasized by a number of lines or is bordered with pothooks. Mudjur also produces prayer rugs with series of niches, as many as nine in different colors. Horizontal lines that enclose a series of small niches or battlements (*maisonnettes*) are characteristic. The full construction with rather deep pile has about 100,000 Turkish knots to the square meter (see illustration on page 47).

The Nigdeh prayer rugs of eastern Anatolia were at first made in the style of the "Transylvanian rugs," with opposed niches and classic ornamentation. The most recent Nigdeh types are certainly prayer rugs in origin, but quite coarse, with niches of remarkably simple conception and very economical decoration. Currently, Nigdeh makes small rugs with massive decoration and chemical colors. The wool, however, is of good quality, with some 80,000 Turkish knots to the square meter.

The so-called Transylvanian rugs originated in Turkey. They have been preserved in the old churches of Transylvania. This good fortune has given us many types of classic prayer rug of the seventeenth century. They were produced in

Bergamo rug. *Turkey, twentieth century, 205 by 118 centimeters. Warp and woof: wool. Pile: wool, 7 millimeters. Density of knotting: 102,000 Turkish knots per square meter. Structure: medium-heavy, grainy, somewhat stiff. Two opposed niches constitute the field, and a square with repeated elements forms the medallion. This frequently used arrangement in the ornamentation of rugs bears the Turkish name of odchalik.*

Melas, Ushak, Makri, Nigdeh, etc. During the Turkish period they entered Europe from the southeast, in the independent principality of Transylvania, which maintained trade relations with the Ottoman Empire. This *émigré* group is important and consists essentially of prayer rugs with two opposed niches and a central linking ornament (medallion), as well as an economical use of arabesques and geometric forms. Structure, knots, ornamentation, and colors are like those of the white-background Ushak rugs.

Other prayer rugs have been made in almost all parts of Asia Minor, but none of them has the exceptional qualities of the types we have discussed.

Turkish rugs of the nineteenth and twentieth centuries are divided into two main groups. The first is the Anatolian (*Ana-doli,* "land of the morning," is the name of inner Asia Minor). This label is applied to all knotted rugs of purely popular make produced in Turkey by peasant families and nomadic herdsmen, as well as small rugs, large rectangular rugs, and carpets. This group also includes prayer rugs. The second group comprises urban products (made by hired workers), as well as rugs made by village communities to meet market demands. These products are offered for sale under the name of their places of origin or the generalized designation of the port from which they were shipped, Smyrna.

Anatolian rugs come in a great many variations of popular art, especially when made for personal use. The ornamentation, mostly still original, is dominated by large geometric forms and highly stylized floral motifs. Figure motifs are not used. Bright, fresh basic colors dominate. The base fabric is wool only or goat hair, which makes for a light, flexible structure. The deep pile, 6 to 10 millimeters long, is made of Turkish

knots, medium to coarse. The knotting thread is most often spun of a kind of shiny wool. Sizes range from bedside mats (*jastik*) to large runners and to small, almost square rugs, including the prayer-rug sizes (*namaslik* and *sedchade*). Because of their ornamentation, coloring, and quality, some Anatolians resemble the Kazak rugs of the Caucasus.

Bergamo rugs are characteristic of Anatolia. Since the beginning of the Ottoman era the inhabitants of the countryside around the towns of Bergamo and Akhissar have been making short and long runners and bedside mats in the old style. The chief characteristic of these products is their strictly geometric ornamentation, with large components. Big squares, octagons, and rhombuses, often in combination, divide the red or pale-yellow and grayish field of the rug. Their outlines are stepped or hooked. In the long pieces they are aligned in three rows; in the small ones they constitute the central motif around which other forms are grouped. In the background, stylized stars, rosettes, and plants are arranged in broad patterns. Contrasting, luminous major colors are used. There are also Bergamo prayer rugs with simply opposed niches that frame a geometric medallion. All these types have a rather deep pile and, on the average, 120,000 knots per square meter (see illustration on page 49).

Konia rugs, from the former residence of the Rum Seljuks and the surrounding area (Beshir, are also typically Anatolian. Those preserved from the sixteenth and seventeenth centuries are prayer rugs with tripartite niches with battlements, hooked fillets, and stylized cruets and plants, or else long, narrow rugs. Their ornamentation consists of zigzag parallel bands that form large lozenges, or also of star medallions aligned in the form of alternating staggered rhombuses with little octagons in arabesques. This design recalls that of the Ushak star rugs. The region's recent productions have remained quite faithful to the style. Thus, the red or greenish-yellow prayer rugs often have a tripartite niche with full decoration and crenellated gable with pothooks. The borders have geometric arabesques with palmette forms or rosettes. The coloration is dominated by red and yellow, with a little blue and green. The really deep wool pile gives these rugs a fullness of structure; there are approximately 140,000 Turkish knots to the square meter (see illustration below).

Yuruk rugs claim a special place among the Anatolians. They are made by the nomadic mountain Yuruk and Gotchebe tribes. Few rugs of popular make have found so much favor as these. This is mainly because of the beauty of their colors with their full tones that flow like precious stones on the brilliant wool. The ornamentation is based on division into lozenges, in which hooked rhomboid motifs appear in constantly different color combinations, diminishing toward the interior. The border is ornamented with serrated leaves and rosettes. Usually narrow and long, Yuruk rugs often have warp threads of goat hair and a deep woolen pile, with an average of 120,000 Turkish knots to the square meter.

Kurdish Anatolian rugs are made by Kurds living in the more remote districts around Bayazid, a town in eastern Anatolia. Usually large, these rugs are found in both broad and narrow formats and normally have three arrow-decorated squares as central ornaments, with all kinds of geometric objects to complete them. They are rather dark in color, like the other Anatolian rugs. The structure is somewhat thin, and the medium-deep, brilliant pile has about 90,000 Turkish knots per square meter.

Eastern Anatolian rugs are made in many parts of central and eastern Turkey. They are sold principally under the names of their places of origin—Karahissar, Karapinar, Maden, Malatya, Ortakoy, etc. Many types have very original

Konia rug. *Turkey, end of the nineteenth century, 306 by 122 centimeters. Warp and woof: wool. Pile: wool, 9 millimeters. Density of knotting: 90,000 Turkish knots per square meter. Structure: full, grainy, rather heavy. Six star medallions in diamond shape are staggered with ten small floral arabesques of octagonal shape. The ornamentation of the field and borders is similar to that of Ushaks with the classic stars. The border should also be compared with that of the Khotan rug (see illustration on page 126).*

varicolored geometric ornamentation, hardly influenced from outside and handed down by tradition century after century in these isolated mountain regions. They include prayer rugs with special or simply suggested niche forms, but principally with two opposed niches that frame a medallion and grouped motifs. Other small rugs have loosely scattered palmettes and rosettes, with heavy arabesques or a large medallion. They often have rather dark colors on a red or blue background. The thick structure, with a deep nap, has 80,000 to 120,000 Turkish knots per square meter.

Karaman rugs, from a southeastern province, are known as *"Kilims"*—that is, woven rugs. They are made of broad bands according to a special way of weaving in which the spools bearing the different-colored wool threads for the motifs are made to pass back and forth through the warp threads. The strips thus produced are then joined to make a rug or blanket. Karaman rugs have flat geometric designs composed of motifs in dark or bright colors. But knotted rugs are also made in this region. Since the turn of the century the Turkish rug factories have not enjoyed the same reputation as before. In part they have lost out to the strong competition of the Persian rug, but their lowered reputation results mainly from a progressive paralysis of artistic ingenuity, leading to the abandonment of personal style in favor of imitations of Persian ornamentation and European designs.

Hereke rugs, from the last sultan's great court manufactory, are the best of Turkey's recent productions. Beginning at the start of the nineteenth century, many rugs of especially fine knotting and in all sizes, with delicate floral ornamentation, were made there. Their structure is thin but resistant; their nap is close and smooth, and their coloring light and luminous. The designs consist of close arrangements of flowers of every knd or of flower motifs taken from more ancient Turkish rugs. But the designers based other creations on motifs of the French rococo. The production also includes beautiful prayer rugs full of flowers and arabesques. On light backgrounds, different tones of violet-red, turquoise blue, or pistachio green always bring out a delicate aura of color. Hereke rugs are knotted with a shiny wool, or often silk, on a base fabric of silk or cotton with fine threads. They represent a more ancient tradition, and today they are especially valuable. They have 300,000 to 400,000 Turkish knots per square meter and sometimes a million knots to the square meter when the Persian knot is used.

Kumkapu rugs owe their name to the Armenian quarter of Istanbul, where they were made in modest workshops toward the turn of the century. They include chiefly costly silk prayer rugs with dense ornamentation in the classic style, composed of arabesques, palmettes, and cloud bands. Verses from the Koran are woven into them in gold and silver thread. The colors are mainly bottle green, ruby red, and golden yellow. These valuable pieces have 400,000 and more Turkish or Persian knots to the square meter.

Panderma rugs are made in the workshop of the town of Bandirma. They are quite small, though some are prayer-rug size. The nap is short to medium, generally of silk, on a base fabric of cotton the threads of which are often colored golden yellow. Their ornamentation is modeled on that of antique rugs, with tendrils, arabesques, and flowers, as well as on that of the classic prayer rugs. Salmon pink, blue-gray, golden yellow, and pistachio green frequently appear in the coloring of the rather old pieces.

Peasant girls in the environs of Sivas, Turkey, weaving a rug. *The loom is a simple frame made of two vertical side pieces and two crosspieces from which the warp threads hang. A wooden slat between alternate warp threads and a wooden stick with which the knots are tied on alternate warp threads serve to separate the warp threads for the passage of the woof threads. The work consists of tying a colored knotting thread (the knot) to a pair of warp threads. When each knotted row is finished, two woof threads are woven and rammed down tight by means of a steel comb (lower right in picture). The balls of wool of various colors are hung up in such a way that the knotter has the thread that she needs readily available.*

The most recent Pandermas have a simpler decoration in light chemical colors. Their structure is tighter, with about 240,000 Turkish knots to the square meter.

Kayseri rugs are manufactured in the town of that name. Rugs and runners of average size, some made in home workshops and many in silk, often have a cotton warp but a woolen woof, which gives them a lighter structure. The ornamentation employs Turkish, Persian, and also Caucasian motifs in rhomboid divisions or in medallion arrangements. A range of soft tones on light backgrounds makes these rugs pleasant and distinguished. The pile is medium-deep, and there are 240,000 Turkish or 320,000 Persian knots to the square meter.

Kirshehir rugs are ranked among the best specimens of the Smyrna group. They are made in the town of Eski-Shehir, southeast of Ankara, in workshops and at home. Ornamentation and coloring are derived from Persian models, making many Kirshehir rugs resemble those of Tabriz. They have medallions on a red background or a simple repeated design of tendrils, arabesques, and palmettes, or the *botah* motif. In Eski-Shehir all sizes of rugs are made on a base fabric of cotton, with an average of 240,000 Persian knots per square meter.

Isparta rugs, called Sparta in the trade, are certainly the best-known Turkish manufactured products of our era. They are made in big establishments in the town of Isparta, not far from Smyrna, and are generally classed among the Smyrna rugs. They have virtually the same characteristics as the Kirshehirs. But they have every possible design, and come in pastels and stronger tones, and in all sizes and qualities.

Sivas rugs were mentioned by Marco Polo in the thirteenth century. Today, these finely knotted rugs of average size are made in the town of Sivas and the surrounding area in northern Anatolia, where peasant families work on them at home. They repeat the ornamentation of older Turkish and Persian types. In structure and coloring they are often deceptively similar to Tabriz rugs. This is especially so when they use the mosaic Herati design fragmentarily with a central piece in the form of a rhombus or a medallion with tracery and palmettes in the ancient style. The dull, smooth, medium-deep wool is knotted on a base fabric of cotton, often with a wool weft. These rugs average 280,000 Persian knots per square meter.

"Smyrna rugs" is the generic market name for almost all kinds made in Turkey, including those produced at home, because all of them are exported to the West through the port of Smyrna. The use of this term resembles the use of Bokhara to describe all Turkoman rugs. Inland from Smyrna the country is still one of the most important centers of rug production, but the output of each different locality has on the whole retained its character. The best-known Smyrna rug—coarse, soft, with deep pile and a heavy medallion in light colors—adopted by the West for decades and appreciated for its low price, furthermore, has never been made in Turkey, but in Greece. Today, almost without distinction, the name of Smyrna is given to all rugs made in Eski-Shehir, Isparta, Sivas, etc. According to their ornamentation, they are then subdivided into "Smyrna-Ghiordes," "Smyrna-Senneh," "Smyrna-Seraband," etc.

Borlu rugs, made in an area near Smyrna in all sizes and intended for export, also belong to the Smyrna group. The deep-piled Borlus are made for the market in Persian, Turkoman, and even Chinese designs. Their base fabric is cotton and they have about 180,000 Turkish or 240,000 Persian knots to the square meter.

11
The Rugs
of the Caucasus

Between the Black and Caspian seas, in the region of the Caucasus, the art of the knotted rug is as old as it is in neighboring Turkestan. The Turkish tribes known as rugmakers appear in the history of the Transcaucasus in the closing centuries of antiquity. We know, for instance, that the Avar tribe of the Lesghians established a kingdom in Daghestan (Avaristan) that, after the domination of the Huns, extended from the fifth to the ninth centuries and as far as eastern Asia, while the empire of the Khazars or Khazori (undoubtedly the predecessors of the Kazaks) extended beyond the Caucasus into southern Russia, as far as Kiev, from the fifth to the eleventh centuries.

The magnificently colored Caucasian rugs were admired in Europe as early as the beginning of the Renaissance. Faithful reproductions in fourteenth- and fifteenth-century paintings show rugs in which the characteristics of style, design, and ornaments are almost identical to those of Caucasian rugs of quite recent times. Such an attachment to old design forms emphasizes the persistence of the past, but it would be unjust to conclude that there had been a general stagnation in the art of the knotted Caucasian rug. For while the ornamental forms were preserved in their individuality in isolated mountain areas and regions peopled by nomads, many regional specialties appeared at the same time in which one can observe a varied stylistic development enriched by a great diversity of types. Thus we note that the Caucasian rugs of the best known of the major antique groups, like the recent types, have many ornamental variants added to the splendor of their colors.

In the antique Caucasian works we can distinguish at least three kinds of classic rugs. The oldest known is the geometric animal-figure rug, often copied in early Renaissance painting in the fourteenth century. Two examples remain, though in fragments. They show a traditional division of fields into series of squares and octagons in which there are animals and birds, most often in pairs and fighting. This ornamentation corresponds to a stylistic tendency of antiquity that was long kept alive in remote areas of the Caucasus. It may be representative of a style of animal ornamentation that characterized antique Turkoman rugs before the Islamic influence.

The second kind is the so-called dragon rug, the ornamentation of which represents a continuing stylistic development of the first group by means of a softening of movement in the base forms with the help of floral motifs. Dragon rugs are massively divided by broad serrated leaves in arabesques, which give an effect of voluminous tendrils. Diagrammatic sections of animal figures and of scenes of violent animal combat, as well as large palmettes, trees, and stylized shrubs, arabesques, cloud forms, tendrils, and flowers, fill the fields of the rhombuses in alternating colors. Spear-shaped leaves, lilies, and palmettes are aligned in the simple, narrow borders. The animal figures (dragons), often much elongated, were later symbolized by mixed figures is the form of leaves, half-animal, half-plant, or by huge S's. The style of the dragon rugs dates from the fifteenth century and continued sporadically until the end of the nineteenth. The third classic group is that of the Caucasian-Persian rugs of the northwest. It came into being in the eighteenth century, after the conquest of the southern Caucasus by Persia under Nadir Shah. New centers arose in which an infinite number of varieties of remarkable rugs emerged. The standard motifs of the already established art of the Persian rug were superimposed on the ancient Caucasian ornamentation. At the same time, through a genuinely Caucasian stylization, a new ornamentation of mosaiclike motifs, always arranged in staggered alternation, appeared. The new Herati and *botah* motifs, as well as different forms of palmettes and medallions, were also introduced. Only the arrangement of concentric medallions was abandoned. Rugs of the Kuba, Karabagh, and Shirvan groups attest to the long-lived influence of this development.

The varieties of Caucasian rugs may be divided into two main groups according to their style and structure. The first group includes those of high or medium-high pile (7 to 12 millimeters) and moderately fine to coarse knotting, from the mountains inhabited by settled tribes of herdsmen. The full structure of these

Daghestan (Darosh) rug. *Caucasus, nineteenth century, 242 by 114 centimeters. Warp and woof: wool. Pile: wool, 7 millimeters. Density of knotting: 132,000 Turkish knots per square meter. Structure: medium-heavy, tight, ribbed. The simple geometric ornamentation, with scattered motifs and small human figures, as well as the border arabesque of leaves treated like the feathers of an arrow, is characteristic of the rugs of the nomads.*

types corresponds to their makers' need for warmth at high altitudes. They preferred large octagonal, square, and diamond figures, with pothooks, in various combinations or in grouped forms, as well as contrasting dark basic colors. Daghestan, Kazak, and Talish rugs are examples. They are almost square, or elongated like runners. The second group comprises rugs made both by townspeople and by peasants. They have a short or medium pile (5 to 8 millimeters) and medium to fine knotting, and they are smooth and thinner. The ornamentation of these types consists of an alignment of small, richly varied geometric forms and of stylized floral motifs with frequent use of larger central motifs, such as medallions. Coloration is very varied. Alongside strong main colors there is a whole range of intermediate tones, as illustrated by Karabagh, Shirvan, and Moghan rugs. They appear in elongated and runner form and in various sizes. The Turkish knot is used throughout the Caucasus. The base fabric is always a wool warp and woof. Only the Shirvan types have a thin cotton thread for the woof. In comparison with the old pieces that retain their standing as valued works of art and antiques, the newer are essentially industrial and heavy.

Baku rugs used to be made in the area surrounding the modern petroleum center of that name, in the Apsheron peninsula. They are elongated specimens, moderately large, or else square. Divided into rectangular fields, the ornamentation usually consists of stepped octagons or polygons, filled with hooklike arabesques, that alternate in light red and yellow ocher. The light-blue background and the white borders are loosely covered with rosettes and hooked shapes. There are also specimens with geometric medallions and tendrils. The prayer rugs have a marked niche with a fully decorated back-

Stepped polygon with latch hooks, Caucasus

ground. The coloring is characterized by a pale tonality unusual in the Caucasus, and which was probably caused by the oil content of the local water. The structure of the Baku rugs is rather loose and light. The low nap on a woolen warp and cotton woof averages 100,000 Turkish knots to the square meter. Surakhani rugs, from the village of that name near Baku, have virtually the same characteristics. These are chiefly prayer rugs with a niche simply suggested by a quadrangular gable, while the interior is strewn with small geometric flowers. Saljany rugs, made in Saljany, on the banks of the Kura, are finer and tighter. They are often shaped like elongated runners. They have varicolored geometric forms in staggered alignment, with rosettes sometimes arranged in a honeycomb pattern; occasionally the *botah* design is found. The border contains diagonals in various colors or rosettes. The Saljany types have strong, bright colors. The medium-deep pile has about 180,000 Turkish knots to the square meter. Farther west from Baku is Shila, where the rather large, rectangular Shilas were made, along with the smaller prayer rugs. The typical ornamentation consists of a staggered alignment of *botah* motifs, often combined with large hexagons that appear also as center and corner pieces and have tendrils with leaves. The coloring on a turquoise-blue or light-red background is in delicate tones, as in

57

Star shape, Caucasus

the Baku types. The smooth, short pile has about 160,000 knots per square meter.

Daghestan rugs, originating in the mountainous northeastern Caucasus on the shore of the Caspian Sea, were made in many types by the Lesghi and Chechen tribes. A honeycomb division of the field with solid motifs or large polygons and formations of stepped stars the whole length of the longitudinal axis usually provide the ornamentation. Many types simply have diagonal stripes in the narrow field. Others have little mosaic motifs of stylized flowers in a staggered arrangement. Their bright colors stand out against the background of blue, natural white, or occasionally, yellow or green. Varicolored ornaments composed of four or six hooked spears arranged in staggered rows are conceived not as a "scorpion design" but as abstract flowers. In the field, again, there are geometric forms and hooked figures as well as little figures of animals and men. The border has serrated leaves with a flower similar to a wineglass or a link

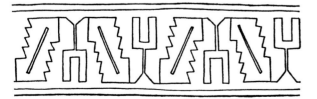

"Wineglass" border, Caucasus

design in various colors made of hooked spears facing or crossing one another, or also, though in a stepped arrangement, triangular leaf motifs or geometric flower calices. Daghestan coloring consists of light major colors, among them much yellow and green. The shapes are almost exclusively long and narrow or almost square. The structure is tight, even hard, because the warp threads are generally fully stretched. The smooth, medium-deep pile is of shiny wool, with about 140,000 knots per square meter (see illustration on page 56). Rugs from Lesghistan, a region west of Daghestan, are called Lesghis and are distinguished from those of the eastern part of the country by finer knotting, a slightly deeper pile, and a smooth underside. There is also much yellow and green in the field. The ornamentation has large squares containing light octagons, with geometric arabesques. Other types have only octagons containing stepped, hooked polygons or large, star-shaped figures. The major motifs contain stylized, varicolored flowers and tendrils. The Lesghis are characterized by particularly vivid coloring. There are also many Daghestan prayer rugs. At the end of the field they have a kind of angular gable that suggests the niche, but the field is always filled with brightly colored, geometric flowers. The white border often contains small octagonal rosettes. There are about 180,000 Turkish knots to the square meter. Derbend rugs are made in the vicinity of the port city of that name, on the Caspian. They are quite coarse, and fairly often, though not as a rule, they have a base fabric of cotton. Ornamentation and coloring resemble those of the Daghestans. The nineteenth century produced a separate Derbend group characterized by designs of large, naturalistic roses, flower bouquets, and garlands. Only the border ornamentation remained geometric. These rugs with

European motifs were ordered from St. Petersburg (now Leningrad) and Moscow.

Karabagh rugs, from the region of that name in the southern Caucasus, show the influence of Persian ornamentation and color. The design consists of geometric figures and often, too, of naturalistic plant and flower motifs, as well as medallions with large mosaic pieces. The coloring consists of various gradations of tints. Characteristic is the violet-red field or the relatively large motifs in field and borders. In addition to the long rugs there are some large, rectangular rugs and runners as long as 25 feet. In the typical Karabagh the more or less busily ornamented field has the so-called pillar medallion, which, with its numerous additions and accretions, extends the whole length of the field, the different parts being connected with one another by a decorative band (the pillar). Other types

have a mosaic design made of angular tendrils with varicolored flowers and leafy arabesques or large escutcheons in staggered alignment, alternating with cartouches in rhomboid shape. The base fabric is wool, the pile is smooth and medium-deep, and there are about 200,000 Turkish knots per square meter (see illustration below). The rugs made in Shusha, the capital of Karabagh, have high-quality ornamentation, often very delicate, with medallions made of minuscule flowers and mosaic pieces or vase and *botah* motifs on a bright, cochineal-red background. Others with a dark-blue background have varicolored tendrils and flowers accompanying a violet-red "shaft" medallion. But the majority have heavier, almost geometric forms. For the Russian market of the nineteenth century, Shusha also produced a number of rugs with roses, groups of flowers, or natural garlands in imita-

Karabagh rug, commonly called "dragon rug." *Caucasus, end of the eighteenth century, 256 by 118 centimeters. Warp: wool. Woof: cotton. Pile: wool, now 5 to 7 millimeters. Density of knotting: 116,000 Turkish knots to the square meter. Structure: smooth, pliable, spare. The ornamentation of this late example of a "dragon rug," with its massive serrated leaves with tendrils around two rhomboid medallions, represents a stage in the development of the "eagle or sword Kazak" (see illustration on page 68).*

tion of the rococo European Gobelins. The structure and coloring resemble those of the Karabaghs. Among the products of various localities in the Karabagh region, Channik and Jabrail rugs deserve mention. They are quite long and generally have a *botah* motif on a blue field. Karadis rugs look much like the Shirvans, but they have a deeper pile and a cotton woof. They have a hooked pillar pattern in staggered rows, the colors of which stand out against a dark-blue field. Shondzores rugs, either quite long or almost square in shape, are also made in this district and have the same ornamentation as the so-called cloud-bank Kazak rugs. The ornamentation consists of two or four large, octagonal medallions in which sinuous wreathed motifs coil in a spiral around a central swastika.

The whole composition, in fact, represents the ancient Turkish symbol for the cloud whirlwind designated also by the word *khani*. These rugs, like the Chelaberds, belong to the major Kazak group (see under Kazak rugs).

Gendja rugs, from the farther outskirts of that city, now called Kirovabad, resemble the Kazaks, though with more variety in ornamentation and choice of colors. Their structure is also finer. This caravan stop between Tiflis and Baku was once the central collection point for all the rugs of the Kazak region. The typical motif of the antique Gendjas is a stepped, hooked polygon usually contained within octagons of changing colors arranged in checkerboard style in the field. This ornamentation is very rich in its variety of colors. There are large, almost square

Gendja rug *(the city is now called Kirovabad). Caucasus, nineteenth to twentieth centuries, 197 by 98 centimeters. Warp and woof: wool. Pile: wool, 7 millimeters. Density of knotting: 106,000 Turkish knots per square meter. Structure: full, somewhat rough and grainy. This type of rug depicted in European paintings as early as the fifteenth century. The ornamentation is closely related to one of the variants of the Khotan rugs of eastern Turkestan (see illustration on page 126).*

rugs with four main large motifs or small, square rugs and long runners with the design arranged in two or four rows. The border contains small octagons or a linked arrangement of motifs, as well as the reciprocal triangular motif. In the center of small rugs there is a large square filled with an octagon, and radiating from this principal motif, geometric forms as well as hooked arabesques. Large rugs have varicolored diagonal stripes with flowers and *botah* motifs. The border contains club-shaped designs or triple crenellations. The colors are sharply contrasting. Gendja rugs vary a great deal. Many have a full, stiff structure; others are looser and soft; still others are thin but tightly knotted. The number of Turkish knots on a base fabric of wool varies from 90,000 to 200,000 (see illustration on page 60).

Kazak rugs are so typical of Caucasian artisanry that the name is used for most of the Caucasian varieties. The various Kazak tribes formerly lived in the southwest Transcaucasus, but most of them emigrated to Kazakstan. Although their rugs are quite alike in character and structure, they vary according to their places of origin. All have in common geometric ornamentation composed in the grand style and the contrast of bright major colors. Their quality is usually thick, full, and tight, though there are other types with coarser knotting and looser structure, as well as still others with a medium-deep pile. The base fabric is of 3-ply warp threads in natural color and, usually, red-dyed woof threads, both wool. The 8- to 12-millimeter pile is often somewhat uneven. As herdsmen and small peasants, the Kazaks prefer to make small, rectangular room rugs and small, nearly square throws, with 120,000 to 200,000 Turkish knots per square meter. A characteristic type is the Bordjalu-Kazak with its small, thick throws

Kazak octagon

and its short, but wide, room rugs. On a madder background they have three plain or hooked massive octagons and rhombuses against a changing field color, arranged as a medallion and enclosing various symbols. Different varicolored ornaments and occasionally little figures of men and animals are arranged in the field. Other Bordjalus have varicolored hexagons in a staggered arrangement as field ornamentation. The blue or white border contains serrated leaves with flowers, rosettes, or pothooks, while the narrow borders are decked with reciprocal battlements (see illustration on page 62). Another type, the Fashralo, is found chiefly as a prayer rug with a suggested niche and a thinner structure. The red field has a geometric background and rosettes. The Karachof-Kazak is either square with a big octagon in the center and four white rectangles, filled with stars, around it, or two white rectangles are arranged lengthwise as major motifs, alternating with three red polygons. The green field has loosely arranged geometric ornaments and figures of animals, and the white border has a chain of pothooks (see illustration on page 63). In Karakli a somewhat different Kazak rug is made. These are usually rather large, long rugs, fairly dense, in which the ornamentation is often composed of flowers and birds faithfully copied from nature. Their medallions, composed of large, coupled geometric forms, extend the whole length of the field, which

would also indicate some Karabagh influence. The Kars-Kazaks come from the area of Kars on the Anatolian border. Most often they have a blue background, and their ornamentation resembles that of the Yuruks. It has a triple major motif composed of rhombuses made of hooked bands in alternating colors, placed in the field with hooked arabesques of yellow, green, and red. The white border has hooked rods and serrated rosettes. The medium-deep pile is rather coarsely knotted. The inhabitants of Luri-Pambak, of Luri and Kurdic origin, make special, smooth-napped rugs. These are rather small, tightly knotted pieces, ornamented with a large octagon with four palmettes and surrounded by geometric flowers. Others have a field with large flowers arranged in a cross, in staggered order. The colors are often very dark, though occasionally pleasantly bright, too (see illustrations on pages 64 and 66). The Lambalo-Kazaks are small, thick rugs with deep pile, often somewhat crowded with simple but mag-

nificently colored decoration. The wide border with many stripes and varicolored motifs around the narrow field is the real ornamentation. In contrast, the Shulaver-Kazak is full of small ornaments in dense arrangements and several colors. Three richly ornamented hexagonal medallions inside squares bounded by the color, with varicolored motifs, divide the long field. In the white border runs a garland of leaves with star-shaped flowers. The medium-high nap is knotted in brilliant wool. The Shondzor, also known as the "cloud-band Kazak," offers rather thick, dense rugs with two to four large octagons of different colors, containing cloud-band motifs grouped in rays, with sinuous shapes and alternating colors. In the center a small square holds a swastika, the geometric form of the symbolic cloud whirlpool of old Turkey. As a whole the primitive symbol of serpentine dark and light cloud bands represents a whirlwind related to the heavenly battle between good and bad weather (or good and bad spirits). This kind of

(Opposite page) Kazak rug.
*Caucasus, nineteenth to twentieth
centuries, 242 by 146 centimeters.
Warp and woof: wool. Pile: wool,
10 millimeters. Density of knotting:
94,000 Turkish knots per square
meter. Structure: full, shaggy,
rather heavy. This rug is
interesting because of the rounded
latch hooks of the diamond medallions and the border arabesque.*

Kazak (Karachof-Kazak) rug.
*Caucasus, nineteenth century, 204
by 116 centimeters. Warp and
woof: wool. Pile: wool, 7 millimeters. Density of knotting:
124,000 Turkish knots per square
meter. Structure: full, tight,
somewhat granular and ribbed.
White rectangles alternate with
red polygons. The border contains
facing double hooks in alternating
colors. The green field is
characteristic.*

Luri-Pambak (Luri-Kazak?) rug. *Caucasus, nineteenth century, 218 by 104 centimeters. Warp and woof: wool. Pile: wool, 9 millimeters. Density of knotting: 114,000 Turkish knots per square meter. Structure: thick, full, soft, slightly ribbed. In the Luri-Pambak district of the Kazak region, some of the population—probably of Luri extraction—makes Kazaks of this type, which are also to be found with an octagonal medallion in rather dark coloring.*

Cloud band

motif is called *khani*. The border is variously ornamented (see illustration on page 67). The Chelaberd type, also called the "eagle Kazak," is usually a deep-pile rug, large and almost square. Its ornamentation, a legacy of the old "dragon rugs," is found in many parts of the Caucasus. It has the so-called spoke medallion, composed of long-stemmed irises grouped radially around a central, cross-shaped motif. Two to four of these medallions in several colors are distributed in the field. There are also pieces with one medallion and two half-medallions in the shape of large, serrated leaves. The border usually contains rosettes along two wavy fillets. The Chelabi are the Turkish tribe that lives in the Gendja khanate (see page 68).

Moghan rugs are related by their ornamentation to the Talish types. They were produced in the Moghan steppe of the southeast Caucasus by the Nogai tribes of Turks. Usually they are in the form of short runners. Design and colors attest to sophisticated taste. Often the whole field of the rug is divided by longitudinal stripes, borders of a sort, which contain geometric forms of small flowers. Other types have stepped polygons in various colors, filled with geometric arabesques and animal figures, or hooked diamonds, as well as polychrome *botah* motifs in alternating rows. The varied coloring is subdued and harmonious. An abundantly used yellow contributes to the luminosity of all the other colors.

The border, often with a yellow background, is sown with abstract flower or leaf shapes. Moghans have a medium nap on a base fabric of wool, with some 160,000 Turkish knots to the square meter.

Cabestan rugs come from the town of Kuba and environs, in the middle of the eastern Caucasus. This is the old khanate of Kubistan, which accounts for the name "Cabestan." These rugs are also classed in the Shirvan group, but as Cabestan Shirvans. Whereas the Cabestan types have more circular ornaments and a tighter base fabric with a ribbed underside because of the arrangement of their warp threads, the Shirvans usually have geometric motifs and a supple, smooth structure. The Cabestans are chiefly runners with a warp of wool (sometimes of cotton) and most often a woof of cotton. The smooth pile measures no more than 4 to 6 millimeters. Beautiful staggered or alternated medallions are characteristic of the ornamentation —often they are combined with flail-shaped cartouches, escutcheon palmettes, and rosettes. In straight or oblique cross form, they are arranged in series of medallions known as cross or flail types. A —multistriped border with an alignment of motifs in the outer band, often with a design like ocean waves (the "running-dog" pattern), is characteristic. Other Cabestan types have a design made of stylized tendrils and flowers, ascending or continuous. Every hue, in dark and light tones, is present in the coloring. There are 180,000 to 260,000 knots per square meter (see illustration on page 69). The Karagatchli type, an almost square corridor rug, has three forms of rhomboid red escutcheons on the bias. Because of their extensions of leaves in arabesques always grouped in fours with long stems inclined in the direction of the whirlwind, they have a stylized swastika shape. The finely knotted

65

Kazak (Kurdish-Kazak)
rug. *Caucasus, nineteenth
to twentieth centuries, 252
by 178 centimeters. Warp
and woof: wool. Pile:
wool, 8 millimeters.
Density of knotting: 98,000
Turkish knots per square
meter. Structure: full,
slightly ribbed, medium-
heavy. Coming from Persia
at the latest in the
eighteenth century, the
Luris and the Kurds moved
into the Kazak region as
a consequence of Nadir
Shah's conquest of the
Caucasus.*

Shondzor rug. *(Karabagh-Shondzor, also called "cloud-band Kazak"). Caucasus, nineteenth to twentieth centuries, 197 by 116 centimeters. Warp and woof: wool. Pile: wool, 8 millimeters. Density of knotting: 96,000 Turkish knots per square meter. Structure: full, pliable, somewhat rough. The light and dark cloud-band motifs framed within the octagonal medallions and surrounding a square containing a swastika, represent the old Turkish symbol of the cloud whirlwind that is related to the combat of the sky and the elements (or of good and evil spirits).*

Karagatchlis have a low, even, velvetlike pile. Konagkend rugs, from the village of that name, have a rather tight structure and relatively deep pile. They have either a grouped ornamentation consisting of a large central piece (octagon, rhombus, or polygon) and radially arranged shapes with scatterings of motifs, or a mosaic design made of angulate tendrils and flowers in latticework, similar to the ornamentation of the Seljuks. The coloring is composed of dark blue with pale green, red, brown, and yellow. The border has latticed arabesques with rosettes. The Perepedil types from the vicinity of Kuba are long runners with a quite hard structure and a ribbed underside. The ornamentation retains much of the "dragon rugs," especially in the flower and leaf motifs in animal forms. The design has little stepped octagons or lozenges aligned on the longitudinal axis, alternating with geometric spiral arabesques in pairs. What is typical is the "rams' heads" aligned on each

side, again a figure in which the animal and floral elements are joined in the ornament. There are also types with flower and plant forms in continuous arrangement, the design of which is related to the Persian Feraghan rugs. Seichur (Kevsur) rugs, from the town of that name, are beautiful but rare. Generally they are runners, with a rather high nap. They are the products of extremely sophisticated work, and their ornamentation can compete with the finest Persian designs. It has aligned medallions, richly subdivided and decorated, consisting of four large palmettes arranged in diamonds and four elongated cartouches set diagonally ("flail medallion"). There are several varieties of pattern and color. Natural-looking roses and garlands are also regional types. The white, narrow border often has the wavy blue-billow motif. Among the hardest in structure, with quite a deep pile, are the Zezhva rugs, from the Kuba region. They, too, are chiefly runners. On a dark-blue or red background they have four or five medallions radiating teeth or cones, hexagonal in shape, and filled with various geometric motifs. At either end of the field there are often large red fan-shaped ornaments. The coloring may sometimes seem rather dark. The triple- or multiple-striped border has very dense ornamentation (see illustration on opposite page). Produced by the Chechen tribes who live in some Kuba villages, Chichi rugs, which are generally small squares, have a low nap and fine knotting. Most have a dark-blue field, but a few are red or white. The ornamentation of the field consists either of large star shapes with stepped borders or of small, stepped and hooked polygons. The ornaments are arranged in staggered and diagonal rows, and their colors alternate. The char-

acteristic middle border has a wavy, looped fillet with pretty rosettes and enlargements that remind one of small oblique flails.

Shirvan rugs were made in many types, from the small prayer rug to the long, 35- by 10-foot rug. The Shirvan region, which has its capital at Soumak and runs between the Kura River and Kuba, is an ancient center of rug weaving. The ornamentation of the ancient Shirvans consists in part of Persian motifs of plants and flowers, palmettes, rosettes, tendrils, arabesques, medallions, and cloud bands, as well as Herati and *botah* designs, but stylized in the Soumak fashion and always in a running alignment. But the design of purely geometric motifs and bright colors dominates. The ornaments are in mosaic style or arranged in beehive diamonds.

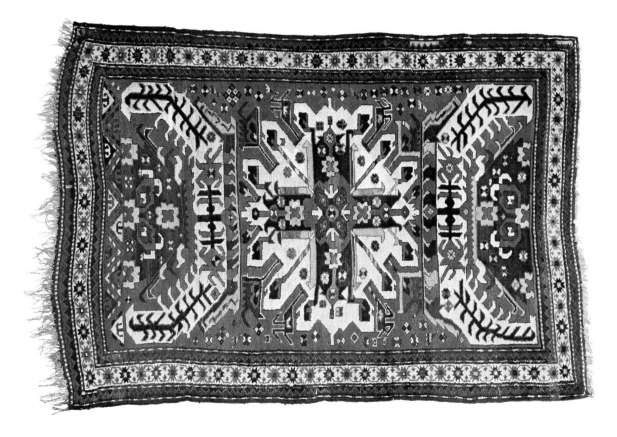

Kuba (Shirvan-Kuba, also called Cabestan) rug. *Caucasus, nineteenth century, 274 by 150 centimeters. Warp: wool. Woof: cotton. Pile: wool, now 4 to 5 millimeters. Density of knotting: 220,000 Turkish knots per square meter. Structure: thin, dense, tight, slightly ribbed. The ornamentation and coloring are characteristic also of the woven Sumaks of the Kuba region.*

(Opposite page) Chelaberd (Karabagh-Chelaberd, also called "eagle or sword Kazak") rug. *Caucasus, nineteenth to twentieth centuries, 205 by 140 centimeters. Warp and woof: wool. Pile: wool, 8 millimeters. Density of knotting: 110,000 Turkish knots per square meter. Structure: full, soft, lightly ribbed. The so-called ray medallion with stylized irises and flanked by half-medallions with serrated leafy arabesques is inherited from the old "dragon rug" of the Caucasus.*

Shirvan rug. *Caucasus, Sejva-Kuba region, nineteenth century, 236 by 124 centimeters. Warp: wool. Woof: cotton. Pile: wool, 5 millimeters. Density of knotting: 266,000 Turkish knots per square meter. Structure: thin, tight, dense, somewhat stiff and ribbed. The crowded, complex ornamentation of the many-banded border is offset by the pleasing alignment of the medallions in the field.*

There are types with large rhombuses, hexagons, polygons, and stars, which generally appear as three medallions aligned along the longitudinal axis. There are also small figures of men and animals. Shirvans comprise short runner types, as well as squares and long rectangles. The warp, often of brown wool, is tight because the fine cotton woof is woven in wave style, and the result is a structure that is always smooth and an underside that is completely even. The nap is short, made of a dull wool, with 160,000 to 200,000 Turkish knots per square meter (see below). An interesting type comes from the Akstafa region. It is characterized by large geometric birds and smaller animal figures aligned along the sides of the field. The birds face each other in pairs and are tiered and staggered in accompaniment with the three central medallions. The same animal ornamentation is used as well in a

Kazak type that naturally has a deeper pile. The ornamentation of the Bidzhov type is especially significant. These rugs come from the vicinity of Shemakha. They have moving forms of flat, markedly serrated leaves with palmettes of massed flowers, and are unquestionably inspired by the style of the "dragon rugs" of the ancient Caucasus. The varicolored motifs, schematically designed, are arranged in an ascending line in close succession on the dark-blue background. Stylized flowered and leafed tendrils make a running pattern in the border (see illustration on page viii). The Shazhli types are quite similar to the large geometric arrangement of the Kazak rugs. These are small throws and long runners with a rather deep pile; large rectangles and octagons are filled with different geometric motifs. Strong basic colors are sharply contrasted, at times with rather light tones. The borders

Shirvan Rug. *Caucasus, nineteenth century, 236 by 122 centimeters. Warp: wool. Woof: cotton. Pile: wool, 5 millimeters. Density of knotting: 236,000 Turkish knots per square meter. Structure: delicate, smooth, tight, dense, and pliable. The rich diversity of motifs scattered haphazardly as well as the human and animal figures around the three rhomboid medallions characterizes this type of Shirvan. The style of the ornamentation is closely related to that of the Qashqai (Shiraz) in southern Persia.*

have fine S scrolls, hooked arabesques, or the intertwined pinks of the Shirvan types (see illustration above). Very rich and varied in ornamentation and fine in structure, the Marasali rugs belong to the Shirvan group. They appear as long runners or as almost-square prayer rugs. Their nap is smooth and short. Their ornamentation consists of two rows of polychrome medallions or rectangles alternating in staggered rows with tree motifs and including small niches. The prayer rugs have a suggested gable, and in the field, diagonally, small varicolored *botah* motifs that are also repeated in the border. The coloring is bright, with a rich use of yellow, frequently employed also in the border, as well as of varied colors. The borders contain small octagons with stars, intertwined pinks, leafy tendrils, etc. The often irregular distribution of colors is characteristic.

Talish rugs, from the southernmost part of the Caucasus on the shore of the Caspian, are always runners, and the style is related to that of the Moghan rugs of the neighboring district. The Talishes also almost always have a broad border arrangement treated in rows made of four to six stripes of an especially beautiful design that frames a narrow field, or an arrangement of longitudinal stripes on the whole surface. The simple but charming and colorful ornamentation consists of rosettes, little stars, and rectangular flowers, delicately designed and arranged in staggered lines, occasionally in a beehive pattern. The narrow field is often without design. It is red and blue. In this case the Talish is called Met-Hane. The structure is similar to that of the Kazaks, but the wool of the woof is occasionally dyed light blue. There are often as many as 260,000 Turkish knots per square meter. The Lenkoran-Talish is a separate type. Its aligned octagonal medallions have serpentine elements added on both sides, resembling wings and filled with the massive serrated leaves of the old "dragon rugs." The coloring, on a black-brown background, tends toward somber tonalities.

73

12

Iranian Rugs

Little is known about the evolution of the rugs of Persia (Iran). The earliest specimens we have go back only to the sixteenth century. There are also, is miniatures, reproductions of rugs of the Mongol period of the fourteenth and fifteenth centuries. These are still purely geometric in their ornamentation.

The foundation of the Safavid dynasty in 1502 launched the glorious period of the classic Persian rug. Over the next two hundred years, highly qualified manufactories in the cities of court life—Tabriz, Kashan, Ispahan, Herat, Kirman—produced the most beautiful rugs in history. But even the earliest of them evidenced a perfection that presupposes centuries of development. Apparently this took place during the Seljuk period, interrupted by the Mongol invasions; as early as 1047, Indian travelers reported that in the Seljuk sultans' cities—Khorassan, Herat, Kirman—hundreds of rugs were being worked. Subsequently, letters from Genoese merchants who had branches in the Crimea confirmed that great manufactories of knotted rugs were part of the "splendor of the Turkoman [Seljuk] court in Tabriz." Also from Tabriz, the

first residence of the Safavids, come some of the most beautiful surviving Persian rugs, including the famous Ardebil Rug of 1539 in the Victoria and Albert Museum in London.

The Safavid rugs of northwestern Persia (Azerbaidjan) are works of considerable size, the ornamentation of which consists essentially of a central medallion, quarter-medallions in the corners, and a tracery of flowered arabesques. The medallions, with eight or sixteen points, made of arabesques, have extensions consisting of escutcheons, cartouches, or lamps. All the ornaments of this concentric division in medallions are arranged in a radial, symmetrical, grouped order in the quarters of the field. The new style of medallion rugs achieved, at the same time, effects of imagery corresponding to those of illuminated books, with representations from nature and lively forms. Among the arabesques, trees, or shrubs, there are also figures of animals of all kinds. When men are shown, they are hunting on horseback ("hunting rugs"). Other types from northwest Persia, dating from the sixteenth century, retain mosaic ornamentation. They have alternating, staggered rows of medal-

Kashan rug—glimpse of the making of an Iranian rug. *Two women are working on a typical Iranian rug whose ornamentation consists of arabesques, palmettes, and rosettes. Only a large, sturdy loom made with long beams is satisfactory for making such rugs. Two strong lateral uprights and two horizontal pieces form a frame on which the warp threads hang vertically. A cylindrical piece of wood running horizontally, to which the warp threads are attached by slipknots, separates alternate warp threads so that the woof thread can be passed between them. Above the heads of the rug weavers are the cylindrical beam and the cartoon with the design that they are executing. The weaver takes two of the warp threads that are side by side and knots around them the woolen pile thread in the proper color, pulls it tight, and cuts it to the desired length with a small knife.*

lions or a mosaic design of spiral tendrils ("arabesque rugs"). There still exist "cartouche rugs" in which there are flagstone patterns of ornamented cartouches and illustrated escutcheons. The border ornamentation of all types consists most often of elongated and round cartouches or arabesques with palmettes and rosettes. The colors are a few major ones—deep blue, deep wine-red, green, brown, and a little yellow. The dull wool is smooth on a base fabric of cotton or silk with 250,000 to 500,000 Turkish or Persian knots to the square meter. As the Ardebil Rug shows, it was possible to make specimens measuring more than 62 square meters.

In the sixteenth century, the city of Kashan, in central Persia, produced admirable silk rugs with exceptionally fine knotting. The dozen specimens surviving generally have asymmetrically arranged motifs of hunting scenes, animals, animal combat, and landscapes copied from nature. The largest, the splendid Viennese Hunting Rug, which is quite long, has an eight-pointed medallion in the middle of picturesque scenes, while the small "animal rugs" create the effect of a varicolored arc of images with animals either alone or fighting among shrubs and stalked flowers, as if in a bird's-eye view. They are classed as picture rugs. The borders contain winged genii or birds alternating with flowered palmettes. The tightly twisted silk made it possible to reach the apex of technique with more than a million knots to the square meter. The mastery of the design and the modulated splendor of the colors with their controlled intensity place these rugs among precious works of art.

Probably originating in Kirman and Shiraz in southern Persia, rugs of the classic period faithfully follow the original design principle. These are rugs with rhombuses of simple or complex ornamentation. The pattern seems to consist only of rows of flowers in rosettes and palmettes, as well as lilies and leaves in arabesques. The design often includes vases or motifs that resemble vases; hence the group is also known generically as "vase rugs." In the simple varieties the division into lozenges is marked by straight, spear-shaped leaves or delicate arabesques. The intensity of luminous colors in the brilliant wool recalls the Caucasian rugs. All the vase rugs are long, with narrow borders, discreetly ornamented. The base fabric of cotton has a markedly ribbed formation of warp threads of hard structure, with 300,000 to 400,000 Persian knots to the square meter.

The beginnings of the classic period of the rug-weaving art also go back to Herat, where in the fifteenth century under the descendants of Tamerlane, a cultural center flourished, the influence of which spread to all neighboring countries. It is not certain that the surviving eastern Persian rugs of the sixteenth and seventeenth centuries came from Herat. The ornamentation of the earliest specimens seems to consist solely of large, curiously lobate flowers in rosettes and palmettes while the system of twelve or eight spirals that serves as the base, symmetrically distributed in running order along the rug, is difficult to recognize. The medallion is never used. Among the ornaments there are isolated or fighting animals, as well as cloud-band motifs in the form of symmetrically ordered loops. Later, the number of spirals was reduced to four and the middle of the field was emphasized by palmettes; the result was the characteristic emergence of a concentric division of the design. Finally, palmettes and rosettes flanked by spear-shaped leaves appeared in the foreground as decorations of the spirals. These were the basis for the evolution of the much-cherished Herati design. The borders are superabundantly ornamented with flowers in a ground of finely designed arabesques. The wine-red field, the moss-green borders, and the yellow motifs and outlines give these rugs a warm coloring. Structure and knotting resemble those of the northwest Persian rugs, but the wool pile is glossy.

Ispahan, which under Shah Abbas (1586–1628) became the new royal residence, certainly produced many classic types, as well as silk medallion rugs without figures but with large abstract palmettes; these are called "Shah Abbas rugs." The famous rugs in the Musée des Gobelins in Paris were undoubtedly made in the royal manufactory in Ispahan. With their design of arabesques composed of layers with four to five steps, they are the unsurpassable summit of the art. They are the acme of the evolution that began to show a clearly deteriorating tendency as early as the beginning of the seventeenth century. The designs lost clarity, and technique degraded style. The consequence was the creation of a new type of Ispahan, known also as the "Polish rug." These are silk rugs of medium knotting on a base fabric of cotton, brocaded on the surface (flat weave) with gold and silver threads. True, medallion compositions were preferred, but because of their eclectic forms, partly brocaded and partly in relief on the knotted silk, most of them became complexes of motifs without any system. Because of the favor that these rugs enjoyed in the West (and in the royal houses of Poland, whence their Polish designation), many examples survive in museums and collections. In spite of a peculiar charm, they show a total abandonment of any feeling for style. Instead of an enrichment of the already thoroughly exploited art of the rug, there was decadence.

Only the upheavals in Persia at the beginning of the eighteenth century led to a stylistic renewal of the art. In 1722, the Afghans destroyed Ispahan, overthrew the Safavids, and took control of a great part of the country. Nadir Shah (1688–1747), a Turkoman prince of Khorassan, drove the Afghans back with the help of his tribes. Then he conquered Herat, Delhi in India, Mesopotamia, and the southern Transcaucasus. He saw the economic importance of the rug industry and encouraged its revival. Thus, a basis was established for a fruitful change in style. Many of the new types with mosaic designs, inspired by popular art, gained worldwide value. Then the rulers of the Kazhar dynasty, which was also Turkoman, added their support to the arts, and starting in 1794, encouraged the revival of the classic rug style. In the second half of the nineteenth century, English, German, and American firms set up new factories in Sultanabad (Arak), Tabriz, Kirman, and Meshed. Hence, the continuation of the art of the Iranian rug. In our own time, too, Iranian rugs are made as often by local artisans among the peasants and nomads as in the urban factories.

Ispahan rugs are still among the best Persian products today. Their graceful ornamentation consists of spirals with flowers and leaves in arabesques of delicate coloring, grouped on a light field around a medallion. Often the round or long, oval medallion is composed of the same tendril work, in broken array, as that which fills the field. Another very ingenious combination is a lacelike design made of staggered flowers. Sometimes the border arrangement overflows with tendrils, which, spilling beyond their frame, weave into the field, or with large *botah* motifs that reduce the size of the corners. Field and border ornamentations interweave, showing the influences of Chinese rugs and Western taste.

The borders are always richly and delicately ornamented. The Ispahans are rather small rugs or long runners of light design and muted coloration. They have a relatively fine but solid structure, with a base fabric of tightly twisted cotton and an even, medium-deep pile of dull-finish wool. They have 420,000 and more Persian knots to the square meter.

Kashan rugs did not return to the market until the middle of the nineteenth century. They are valued for their precisely designed ornamentation that emulates classic models. Round or oval medallions made of arabesques, with extensions and matching decoration in the corners, usually divide the field. The full red, violet, or dark-blue field is filled with spirals bearing flowers with palmettes and in rosettes. Sometimes there is no tendril work, and the medallion remains isolated on a field called a "mirror." Occasionally, too, the Kashan has palmettes in escutcheons in staggered alignment, cartouches, or groups of floral and arabesque motifs. More recent examples often have complex motifs that recall the "Polish rugs." The border contains undulate tracery with palmettes or combinations of groups of flowers. The coloring is dominated essentially by a range of reds, or violet-blue. The general effect is never varicolored. These are medium-size to large rugs, or runners. The base fabric consists of finely twisted cotton thread with a slightly tiered warp and a blue woof. The smooth pile is made of fine wool, usually not very shiny, with an average of 360,000 Persian knots per square meter. There are smaller Kashan rugs of silk, and prayer rugs, also of silk. Their ornamentation is delicate and detailed because of the fineness of their knotting. In the crowded play of arabesques there are also figures of animals and birds. The prayer rugs have niches with purely floral decoration, but they also have beautiful arches supported on columns. A wealth of tendrils loaded with flowers, trees, and bushes creates an atmosphere of boundless joy. The colors are delicately graduated and, of course, lighter and softer on silk. Warp and woof are of silk, or occasionally, of fine cotton thread. The shallow pile has 600,000 and more Persian knots to the square meter. Names such as Kork-Kashan, Arun, and Natan apply to coarser qualities of Kashan production (see illustrations on pages 79 and 80).

Khorassan rugs, from that eastern Iranian province, are hardly ever encountered on the market today under that name. A few decades ago they were still fairly often found in the antique elongated *kelezh* form. Often they had a large mosaic geometric design. In other types there were cloud bands, palmettes, and spear-shaped leaves in abundance, or also the Herati pattern repeated. They also had the *botah* design on a reticulated arabesque ground or various flowered rosettes in a staggered arrangement (*mask*). Modern Khorassans are chiefly manufactured products, from the following areas. The best known are the Mesheds, from the capital of that province. The characteristic ornamentation of these rugs of rather sober coloring is the medallion in arabesques, a starred shape with eight or sixteen points and in large quarters in the corners of the field. Occasionally, the medallion appears on an even, violet-red ground, but usually in the middle of a dense array of flowered arabesques. All types have a broad border made of a number of richly ornamented stripes. The coloring is dominated by a special violet-red, with blue, in a rather dark tone. Some types with light backgrounds have a relatively varicolored floral ornamentation with a small medallion. Although the base fabric is of cotton, the structure is especially flexible. The manufacto-

Kashan rug. *Iran, mid-twentieth century, 206 by 132 centimeters. Warp and woof: cotton. Pile: wool, 6 millimeters. Density of knotting: 380,000 Persian knots per square meter. Structure: dense, smooth, finely ribbed, with the toughness of leather. Here one of the new departments of Kashan manufacture has been used for the ornamentation, quite removed from the usual arabesques and flowers. The style is reminiscent of the "Polish rugs" of the seventeenth century.*

Kashan prayer rug. *Iran, twentieth century, 180 by 140 centimeters. Warp and woof: silk. Pile: silk, 5 millimeters. Density of knotting: 812,000 Persian knots per square meter. Structure: very delicate, thin, smooth and pliable. Ever since the sixteenth and seventeenth centuries, Kashan has had a tradition of weaving extremely delicate silk rugs.*

ries of Meshed, formerly the residence of Nadir, Shah, produce rugs of all sizes, but runners are infrequently come by. The deep pile is made of wool from the Khorassan region with a silky shine, but rather supple, with some 280,000 Turkish or Persian knots per square meter. The best Meshed in the Moud, with meticulous, delicate design and knotting. Its smooth, medium-deep pile is of sturdy wool with more than 350,000 Persian knots per square meter. Although more coarsely knotted and designed, the Darosh, from the mountainous area of that name, is also well made. It is a tight rug with a deep pile, often very large, gaily decorated with imaginative mosaic designs made of rather large floral ornaments. Sabzawar rugs, from that city in western Khorassan, resemble the Masheds in style and quality, but are independent in their ornamentation and coloring. They have medallions and tendrils, and often a mosaic design made of escutcheon palmettes or lozenge formations composed of arabesques with flowers on a light-red background, in luminous tones of blue, green, heliotrope, yellow, etc. The medium nap has some 220,000 Persian or Turkish knots to the square meter. In the Khorassan rugs the Turkish knot is customarily called *turkibaff*, whence such a name as Meshed-Turkibaff. The town of Kashmar, formerly Turkish, produces the coarsest of the Khorassans. The ornamentation consists of a division into a stylized medallion on a large scale or of somewhat heavily designed floral motifs. The tightness of their structures makes these rather darkly colored rugs quite resistant to wear. They also come in very large sizes, with a deep pile. They have about 160,000 Turkish knots to the square meter. Birjand rugs have been made in that area since ancient times. They are long, with *botah* or Herati designs. The ornamentation of the new

rugs, on the other hand, consists of medallions and arabesques in strong colors. In structure they belong to the Meshed group. The Quain rugs, from mountainous Quainat, south of Meshed, used to be renowned for their fine Khorassan style; they were long rectangles and had mosaic ornamentation in light and balanced tones. Modern Quain rugs have an oval medallion form sparingly ornamented with arabesques, which runs the whole length of the field because of its added elements. The light-red background is often plain. The medium-deep pile is made of glossy wool with 200,000 Turkish or Persian knots to the square meter.

Naïn rugs were formerly included with the Khorassans, but they are a separate group because the factory in the town of Naïn, east of Ispahan, produces the finest knotted rugs made today. Their ornamentation consists of delicate medallioned arabesques with vases in added elements and also ingenious combinations of arabesques with flowers and *botah* motifs of great liveliness, without a medallion. In the delicate articulation of its design and the balance of its colors, the Naïn stylistically resembles the Ispahan. The range of colors of these two types is the richest among the Iranian rugs. Naïn rugs are rather small, and the runners are of various sizes. They also include very beautiful prayer rugs in which the niche is suggested by the use of an ascending ornamentation. The thin base fabric of cotton or silk and the rather low nap, flat as a mirror, in fine wool (often with silk threads), make for a light, flexible, but firm structure, with 560,000 to 900,000 Persian knots to the square meter.

Kirman rugs, from the ancient southeastern center of Iranian rug weaving, now as a rule have rococo medallions in the middle of a solid-color field. The evenly articulated floral orna-

Kirman silk carpet (Kirman). *Iran, nineteenth century. 270 x 140 centimeters. Warp and woof: silk with cotton. Pile: silk, 5 millimeters high. Density of knotting: 460,000 Persian knots per square meter. Structure: somewhat reped, firm, thin, light. The modestly articulated classical design and the softly glimmering colors on the silk emanate beauty and restfulness, and for this one can choose to overlook the somewhat irregular form of the carpet.*

mentation of the borders is attached like a large crown to the medallions. Thus, the boundary between field and border is removed. This style was introduced into French Savonnerie rugs and later into those of China. The preferred base color of these rugs is a light green or a violet-red. Other types in this style have a design of little flower groups similar to *mille fleurs* on a natural-white background. Again, the border ornamentation spills over into the field and partly merges with its decoration. The colors, which are restricted to light tones, include violet-red, Nile green, and light and dark blue. Kirman rugs have a dull wool pile on a base fabric of cotton, averaging 240,000 Persian knots per square meter. Laver (Ravar)-Kirman and Eski-Kirman are the names given to the oldest rugs produced in this center and its environs and not yet influenced by Western taste. Next to the Tabriz, these rugs display the most varied ornamentation. Yezd, Ravar, Mahan, Zhupar, and similar rugs have divisions in lozenges made of spear-shaped leaves with palmettes, small, square "flower beds," lines of flowering trees alternating with cypresses, and animal and hunting motifs around a medallion, large *botah* and Herati motifs in staggered alignment or intermingling, and ornaments of tightly coiled arabesques. Numerous types have a large niche in which tendrils or flowered branches rise from vases and support birds. There is also the "figurative rug," with men and animals in asymmetrical arrangement under trees, plus many others. The antique Kirmans were knotted on a base fabric of cotton, with a shallow pile, glossy wool, and variable knot density. Their colors are usually very bright.

On the one hand, the Tabriz rugs carry on the northwest Persian tradition of the art, and on the other, they have the ornamentation of all the important Iranian centers. The Tabriz fac-

tories, both indigenous and European, have been making medium-size to huge rugs of different qualities since the end of the nineteenth century. Particularly characteristic types have baroque, divided medallions with a tracery of plant motifs quite close to nature, or patterns that have already become half-geometric. There are also hunting rugs and animal rugs in the old style, with or without medallions, occasionally of silk. Then, too, there are "garden rugs," with canals and pools in bird's-eye view serving as a frame to square flower beds or copses, as well as various "tree rugs." Examples with arabesques and cartouches are likewise esteemed. The ornamentation makes free use of very strong stylization or geometrization of floral designs handed down by long tradition. The demand for change imposed by a constantly growing export trade has led to the production of exact imitations of antique models as well as the creation of new patterns responsive to almost all stylistic tendencies. Nowhere else does one find such diversity of types. The Herati design is also frequently used in a hexagonal central piece with corner elements, or also around a circular medallion. The centrally arranged types, or those with mosaics of fine wreathed or spiral arabesques filling the field with varying density, are particularly rich in style. The border usually contains two arabesque or undulant movements with alternating palmettes, rosettes, and leaves. While antique Tabriz rugs most often have strong vegetable colors, the later rugs and those produced today are done in light tones of chemical colors. The background is tawny, red, flat blue, or natural white. Tints are used in various gradations, in a general blue-red combination. Tabriz rugs and runners have a relatively short, even nap as a rule. The wool, its glow slightly dulled, is knotted on a base fabric of cotton with a slightly ribbed underside and an average of 220,000 Turkish or

260,000 Persian knots to the square meter. A characteristic of the ornamentation of Tabriz rugs is classic palmettes and rosettes often used in twelve to sixteen different forms in the same piece. Beautiful smaller silk rugs are also made in Tabriz, generally with the Turkish knot. The rugs made in the nearby locality of Khoj resemble those of Tabriz. However, they have a thicker structure with a somewhat mixed glossy wool nap, coarser knottings, and ornamentation that uses fewer bright colors. Sarand rugs, with geometric main motifs and finely stylized flowers, as well as little animal figures, are, in contrast, fine and special. They have a medium-deep pile of brilliant wool with about 300,000 Turkish knots to the square meter, and are frequently quite long rectangles.

Sultanabad rugs have been made since the end of the nineteenth century in factories founded by Englishmen in the town of Arak, formerly called Sultanabad. These are medium-size to very large rugs, with a pile 8 to 10 millimeters deep, tightly knotted on a base fabric of cotton. They are marketed under the names of villages and areas that produce famous rugs. Aside from the Mahadshiran rugs of non-Persian design for export to America, the ornamentation of the Saruk-Sultanabads has flowered motifs and large spiral tendrils with palmettes, rosettes, and animal figures, and usually no medallion. The Mir-Saruk has small *botah* motifs in a staggered arrangement on a blue or cream background, and the borders of the Saraband rugs. The design of the Mahal-Saruk usually resorts to the ornaments of the Feraghan and Mahal rugs, from the environs of Arak. Most frequently these are small mosaic motifs of palmettes, rosettes, and leaves, as well as the Herati motif. There is no criticism to be made of the quality of these rugs, with about 260,000 Persian knots to the square meter, for everyday use, but they no longer have much kinship with the art of rug weaving.

Saruk rugs from the western region of Feraghan get their name from the village where for centuries home workers have made very fine, small knotted rugs with a specially animated and ramified ornamentation composed of arabesques and flowers. They have round or lozenge-shaped medallions of ingenious conception and different patterns in the corners on a field so abundantly filled with arabesques that its dark-blue or rust-red bakground is almost totally hidden. The colors are moderately varied; the admirably ornamented borders are often moss green. The almost rigid structure consists of a base fabric of thin cotton and a low, even nap of glossy, sturdy wool. It is not unusual to find as many as 400,000 Turkish or Persian knots to the square meter. Astana and Teramis, which are nearby, produce similar rugs, which often have the Herati or *botah* design in the form of a miniature, or small rosettes of flowers in a staggered arrangement (*mask*) on a light-red and natural-white background.

Since the eighteenth century the Feraghan rug, from the area between Arak and Kashan, has ranked among the best home-worked products (peasant artisanry) of Iran. The various mosaic designs of the antique rugs, of which there are some twenty variants deriving from one another, are generally called Herati, in spite of a great wealth of forms and related variants in which the Herati motif is often used only in the arrangement of the smaller elements. The Feraghan is characterized by the close alignment of its repeated motifs and its muted color. These quiet rugs with their great style seem to rearrange their design according to the position from which one views them. Sometimes a basic pattern in diagonals dominates, sometimes one that is round or square, and so on. But there are also double cartouches composed of elements in angular arabesques, beehive forms, and diamonds filled with rosettes, spear-shaped leaves, and flowers, which also create an infinite mosaic design. Smaller rugs have long tripartite medallions or a tree of life in a full ascending motif. The borders are ornamented with angular palmettes, leaves, or rosettes on a light-yellow or mineral-green background. The field is blue, copper-red, or natural white. The coloring consists of yellow, red, green, light blue, and brown, very equally divided. Shapes tend to be elongated. The medium nap on a base fabric of cotton has 160,000 Turkish knots to the square meter (see illustration below).

The Mahal rug also comes from various villages in the area of Arak (Mahalat). It is coarser but often very beautifully colored. On a blue field there are large Herati motifs around a central rhomboid piece, a coarser medallion in arabesques with tendril work on a red background, or large palmettes and flowered scrolls. The border contains angular or stylized palmettes, flowers, and leaves joined by the play of arabesques. The coloring is in luminous tones. The dyes are often vegetable—light red, light green, and light yellow. The rather deep pile is of a glossy, somewhat brittle wool, on a base fabric of cotton with blue woof threads. A looser kind of Mahal, slightly like a rag rug, is called Muskebad-Mahal, though that area produces excellently knotted rugs in the traditional Joshaghan design (large rosetted flowers).

Teherans, from the royal manufactory set up in the provincial and residential capital in the Kajar period, are finely knotted rugs of the neoclassic school. They frequently employ the antique ornaments, which are distinguished plastically by the precision of a light, meticulous design, but often, too, there are new, confused designs without style and overcrowded with forms. On certain prayer rugs especially, these create an irritatingly extreme effect. The ornamentation usually consists of compositions of medallions and leafy tendrils, or rows of stylized flowers with short arabesques. There are also garden and tree models. The coloring is moderately varied on a blue, violet-red, or cream back-

Feraghan rug. *Iran, Feraghan region, nineteenth century, 225 by 105 centimeters. Warp: wool. Woof: cotton. Pile: wool, 6 millimeters. Density of knottings 130,000 Turkish knots per square meter. Structure: tight, smooth, pliable.*

ground. Nevertheless, it has strong contrasts. Rugs of all sizes are made in Teheran. The even, medium nap of tough wool is knotted on a base fabric of cotton or silk with 320,000 and more Persian knots to the square meter.

Veramin rugs are the products of home workshops south of Teheran. They are excellently knotted and refreshing to look at, their designs having a purity of style with light forms and colors. Their ornamentation has infinite mosaics of rosettes, palmettes, and flowers in alternating colors, arranged in wavy lines forming diamonds. Other types have variants of the continuing mosaic design. They consist of highly stylized flowers or purely geometric motifs. The border contains arabesques or rosettes. Veramin rugs come as long rectangles or squares as well as runners, with a blue-red-white coloring and a medium nap on a base fabric of cotton, ranging to 330,000 Turkish knots per square meter. Semnan rugs come from the locality of that name on the edge of the salt desert in an oasis east of Teheran. They are long rectangles and runners and have classic decoration. Often they are arranged with a medallion with tendril work on an ocher background, or simply in spirals with flowers. In their ornamentation, their delicacy, and their structure they resemble the rugs of Naïn and Ispahan.

Bijar rugs, from the town of the same name and the villages of the Gherous district between Senneh (Senendij) and Zenjan, have a tight woof and a rather deep pile that make them the thickest knotted rugs. Their structure is often as stiff as a board. Their ornamentation is especially diverse. Medallions composed of arabesques or in hexagonal form with added elements appear as frequently as the stylized Herati and *botah* motifs. There are types with flower and tendril designs as well as arabesques and diamonds filled with palmettes and vases. The field is usually dark blue, deep red, or a camel's-hair color, and the rugs are moderately varicolored. Usually the border contains arabesques with palmettes. The town-made Bijar comes in all sizes. The base fabric of the smaller pieces is all wool; larger ones have a cotton warp. The firm, high nap (10 to 12 millimeters) has 180,000 Turkish knots to the square meter (see illustration on page 88). Gherous rugs, made by the essentially Kurdish village population, have a similar structure but are smaller. Their ornamentation has large geometric rosettes—with angular motifs—or other stylized flower-leaf motifs in continuing mosaic (*do-gule, mini-khana*). The knotting is often very fine.

For many years the rugs of Senendij (Senneh) have been among the finest and most celebrated productions of the weaving and knotting craft of Iran. They are made in the town and surrounding countryside of Senendij by a population made up principally of Kurds. The preferred ornamentation is the Herati pattern with small related elements, most often with a rhomboid or hexagonal motif in the center and at the corners, like the offset alignment of the *mir* motif, in large or small scale. Equally common are fine diagonal divisions with tendrils and also a design based on flowers and palmettes. The border shows almost geometric palmettes on arabesques and angular wave patterns. The colors of antique Senendij rugs have a pleasant softness. Densely covering the cream-colored field, the numerous motifs make a strong impression on one, while the colors of more recent examples of these rugs are violent and frequently somewhat dark. The rugs produced today have also cartouche and geometric shield designs. The fabric of the rug is very thin, the reverse side being strangely grainy because the woof thread is passed tightly through the warp threads. The pile ranges from short to medium-long on a cot-

Bijar rug. *Iran, early twentieth century, 220 by 140 centimeters. Warp: cotton. Woof: wool. Pile: wool, 8 millimeters. Density of knotting: 168,000 Turkish knots per square meter. Structure: thick, hard, tight, ribbed on the back along the warp threads.*

ton or thin silk fabric, and the knotting runs from 260,000 to 600,000 Turkish knots per square meter. (It is impossible to discover why the Persian knot bears the name Senneh [Senendij], a place where it has never been used.) The woven rugs of Senendij, which are also called Do-Rouja (two faces), are the finest of the Orient. They have the same ornamentation as the Senendij rugs.

There are various types of Kurdish rugs with geometric or highly stylized floral ornamentation, in dark but luminous vegetable dyes. On a base fabric of wool, they have a deep, glowing pile, made of good wool knotted in medium to coarse Turkish knots. Almost square passageway and short room rectangles are to be found. Depending on their origins, they are called Karaghos, Goltok, Soughbulag, Gherous, and frequently, Mosul. They are made by nomadic or seminomadic Kurdish tribes.

The Lur rugs of the nomadic tribes in the western part of Iran called Luristan have a geometric ornamentation of related forms of rhombuses or hooked hexagons, large medallions with added hooked elements, trees, stylized plants in a staggered alignment, etc. Frequently, small animal figures are scattered throughout the design. The borders show motifs of serrated leaves or octagonal rosettes. Three or four dark hues derived from vegetable dyes, with a yellow-orange and a dark green appearing most frequently, are used against a dark-blue or rusty-red field. The base of the fabric is almost always wool with the warp often of cotton or goat hair. The very deep pile contains about 140,000 Turkish knots per square meter. Lur rugs are found in large sizes, long runners, and long rectangles. Ispahan-Lur, Khorremabad-Lur, and Kermanshah-Lur with cotton warps and tight knotting are produced in these towns and their environs.

Shiraz rugs are produced by settled or nomadic Turkish tribes in the villages around Shiraz, the former capital of Farsistan in southwest Iran. The Qashqai and Turki are the best known, but they have always been especially different. They have the characteristics of nomadic art and possess many traits related to the Turkoman and Caucasian rugs. Ranging from mats (*pushti*) to medium-size rugs, they are all made on the simple horizontal loom, with the base of the fabric invariably wool and the warp sometimes of goat hair. The ornamentation generally consists of an assemblage of variegated phantasmagoric forms, geometric symbols, shrubs, flowers, rosettes, stylized palmettes, and small animal figures scattered about—often quite densely and asymmetrically—in the field and in the principal motifs. The dark-blue field is divided by large geometric forms or generally by three lozenge-shaped medallions arranged along the longitudinal axis. Or the field may be occupied by staggered octagons, hexagons, or lozenges in a network pattern. Other types have a mosaic design of flowers, roosters, or large *mir* (tree of life) motifs arranged on the diagonal. The border contains geometric arabesques with rosettes or other stylized elements (*achkali*). A brownish red dominates the moderately varied coloring. The luminosity of the mostly vegetable colors of the motifs is heightened by outlining in yellow. The structure may be thin and light or compact and medium-heavy, yet qualitatively very different. The short to medium-long pile has from 80,000 to 240,000 Turkish or Persian knots per square meter. The Gabeh is a dense variety with geometric motifs. Certain types of particularly delicate Shiraz are called Mecca-Shiraz (see illustration on page 92).

The settled and nomadic Turkish tribes of Afshars are found between Shiraz and Kirman

Kurd carpet (Souhbulag). *Iran, nineteenth century. 216 x 125 centimeters. Warp and woof: wool. Pile: wool, 8 millimeters high. Density of knotting: 166,000 Turkish knots per square meter. Structure: full, firm, somewhat reped, almost heavy. On the deep blue ground here, there is a remarkably elaborate tendril-blossom pattern in handsome colors. A masterpiece of the seminomadic Kurds.*

and produce Afshar rugs. The nomadic herdsmen knot rather small, thick rugs and almost square rugs for passageways on a base fabric of wool in Turkish knots. The geometric forms in dark colors generally appear on a red field— staggered medallions with accompanying related motifs or different flat ornaments repeated in loose alignment. An angular arabesque in a wave pattern without much other decoration runs through the natural-white border. The rugs of the people of the villages situated along the shores of Lake Niris, the Niris-Afshar, have a cotton warp, a woolen woof, and a close-sheared woolen pile with a silky luster. Repeated in a continuous alignment on a light-red or cream field, the design consists of bouquets of roses or small variegated flowers copied from nature. Sirjan rugs, from the town of the same name

(formerly Saidabad), are large and frequently quite long. They have a close design of flowers copied from nature set in a sand-colored field and often with a lozenge-shaped medallion. Frequently one finds among the moderately varied colors a light violet-red. The medium-deep pile is knotted on a cotton fabric with 240,000 Persian knots per square meter. The Abadeh rug of the northern Afshar region is similar in quality. Its field is divided by beveled corners and a central hexagonal motif. Small, variegated ornaments cover all the parts as in the Qashqai rugs.

Only in the course of the last decades has the rustic and robust quality of the knotting of Bakhtiari rugs been recognized. They are made in the villages south of Ispahan by the Bakhtiari tribe. These are rather thick rugs, available in all shapes and sizes, the knotting running from

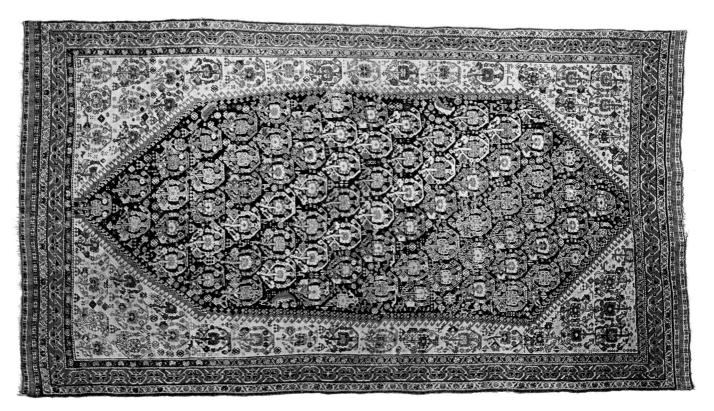

Qashqai rug. (commonly called Mecca-Shiraz). *Iran, early nineteenth century, 274 by 146 centimeters. Warp and woof: wool. Pile: wool, 5 millimeters. Density of knotting: 280,000 Persian knots per square meter. Structure: thin, smooth, slightly granular, and delicate. The floral botah ornamentation is an especially delicate design, and the balance of the coloring assures these nomadic rugs a classical value.*

average to coarse in wool on a base fabric of cotton. They present a very diversified division of the field in a tile pattern filled with trees, shrubs, and stylized flowers, or with vases and figures of birds. The medallion worked in arabesques and the shield and cartouche designs are equally common. All hues may be found among the fresh, vigorous colors, and they are used against a red or natural-white field. There are many variants in a range of qualities. The density of the knots varies from 60,000 to 200,000 Turkish knots per square meter. The most tightly knotted Bakhtiari rugs are called *bibibaff*.

Joshaghan rugs used to be made in large formats in designs with large floral rosettes and undulating arabesques in lozenges. The new rugs are throws and runners. On a rust-red field they have a lozenge-shaped medallion, with a staggered arrangement on the field of palmettes, shrubs, and geometric flowers in dark shades. Similar rugs come from Murdkhakar, to the north of Ispahan. Their ornamentation consists of small lozenges composed of various shrubs, flowers, and arabesques in a repeated pattern, without a medallion. Both these stylish rugs have medium-deep pile, knotted on a base fabric of cotton, with at least 280,000 Turkish and Persian knots per square meter.

Kum rugs, from the holy city of Kum in west-central Persia, are bright and pleasant with a clean, ambitious design and balanced colors. *Mir* motifs in a staggered arrangement or in longitudinal rows, vases with bouquets of flowers, or various related plants are frequently used for ornamentation. Equally common is the division of the field in a checkerboard pattern with lozenges containing a variety of designs as well as a latticework pattern formed of arabesques of flowers and leaves. In such cases the border is treated differently. Strong colors alternate with

pastel tones to give a plastic effect. The field is natural white, light red, or blue. Kum rugs come in normal proportions or as long runners. They have a level pile of medium depth on a base fabric of thin cotton, with 220,000 to 400,000 Persian knots per square meter. The rugs produced in the neighboring locality of Saveh resemble the Kum rugs (see illustration on page 96).

Most Hamadan rugs come from the remoter environs of this ancient city where tens of thousands of knotted rugs have long been made. The different villages and tribes have their own types of design. The antique Hamadans are throw or longish room rugs that have a number of hexagonal medallions filled with Herati motifs and connected with latch hooks. They have surfaces in partly natural or dyed camel's hair. The most recent Hamadan rugs, which come in all sizes and shapes, have a central hexagon and beveled corners; these are known as Ekhbatana rugs. The field is either occupied by small ornaments or is a solid-red or camel's-hair color (*shuturi*). The base fabric consists of a cotton warp and a woolen woof. The pile is even and of average depth, with an average of 240,000 Turkish knots per square meter. Other types in room size and runners and with various kinds of ornamentation are known as Kharak, Anjilas (Indjelas), and Bordjalu. Other examples of tight and loose knotting belong to the Hamadan group. These are the Goudjan and Khamseh rugs and the rather delicate Tafrish with a medallion in arabesques, and the Malair with varied ornamentation. Finally there are the very special Lilihan with flowered tendrils and bouquets, the Maslavan with a serrated medallion and linked rosettes, the coarser Shasevan, whose flowers are arranged in squares and circles, the Zenjan (Sendjan) in a large checkerboard style, and the strictly geometric Viss with its dark col-

Bakhtiari carpet. *Iran, mid-twentieth century. 210 x 135 centimeters. Warp and woof: cotton. Pile: wool, 10 millimeters high. Density of knotting: 114,000 Turkish knots per square meter. Structure: full, firm, coarse, heavy. With this relatively coarse carpet, the almost classical rest of the design coupled with the warm, friendly coloration creates a particularly harmonious effect.*

Kum rug. *Iran, mid-twentieth century, 210 by 140 centimeters. Warp and woof: cotton. Pile: wool, 6 millimeters. Density of knotting: 342,000 Persian knots per square meter. Structure: dense, smooth, delicate, and tough as leather. The finely knotted Kum rugs with their light and joyous colors possess a design of classic style in which we encounter renewed decorative elements that are modern in appearance in spite of old ornamental elements.*

ors. They are all invariably rather small throw rugs, short room rugs, and runners of various lengths on a base fabric of wool or cotton with a pile that is average to deep, with between 90,000 and 180,000 Turkish knots per square meter.

The Sarabend (*mir*) rugs of the region of Sarawan south of Hamadan always have the *botah* (pear or almond) motifs about the size of an egg. The motifs are staggered and alternate from row to row. The field is red, blue, or cream. Sarabend rugs are available in all shapes. The generally deep pile is knotted on a base fabric of cotton with 120,000 to 260,000 Turkish knots per square meter. The more delicate Mir, from Mirabad, has much smaller pear motifs and sometimes a lozenge-shaped medallion.

Heriz rugs, from the city of the same name and the villages of the Bahkshaish region in northwestern Iran, have a pattern based on a largely stylized, elongated medallion on a rust-red or blue field, with a quarter-section of the medallion repeated in the corners against a white background. The dense, semigeometric ornamentation consists of large, serrated tendrils, flowers, leaves, and palmettes in the principal colors, but understated. The border is occupied by an angular wave pattern and palmettes or by stylized flowering shrubs. Some of the oldest Heriz rugs have a commonplace ornamentation in light colors. The shapes run from rectangular to almost square, with sizes to 457 by 732 centimeters. Characteristic of these rugs is the very dense structure on a strong cotton warp. The pile is deep and made of a robust wool, with 160,000 Turkish knots per square meter. Delicate silk rugs are also produced in Heriz. These have an oval medallion with added designs coming out from the medallion or with other ornaments. The most delicate of the Bahkshaish rugs is made at Ahar, with circular forms.

The coarsest Heriz come from the villages of Joraghan, Gorevan, and Mehrevan. The Karaja rugs from the mountainous region of Karahan are closely related to the Heriz. These are throws, room rugs, and runners that resemble the Heriz in ornamentation and quality while at the same time having also numerous Caucasian patterns and motifs. They have three or more geometric principles arranged like medallions along the longitudinal axis. The Barjed is a coarser type with Kazak ornamentation, and the Lamberan is finely knotted with a sharp design and close pile.

Karadagh rugs have a character that is imposed by the bordering region of the Caucasus. The ornamentation is sometimes Caucasian, sometimes Persian. The structure of the long and room-sized rugs—ranging from 91 by 274 centimeters to 274 by 732 centimeters—frequently has Caucasian traits. Large geometric medallions are repeated, sometimes in pairs, three to five times on the lengthened red or blue field. Floral ornaments, stylized tendrils, and small geometric forms with animal figures in a repeated design are equally prevalent. Fresh, lively colors dominate the coloration of the rugs. The border generally carries an arrangement of variegated rosettes with serrated leaves. The pile is rather deep, with 90,000 to 220,000 knots per square meter. Some of the Karadagh rugs are known as Ghafgaz (Caucasian). The Meshgin, which is generally made as a room rug, and the Sarab with its geometric ornamentation and high-quality workmanship, belong to this group, just as the rich and varied Ardebil rugs are technically and stylistically related to the Shirvan rugs. Sometimes thick and rustic, sometimes thin and fine, these types represent the most heartening production of the present-day settled and nomadic Iranian artisanry.

13

The Rugs of Central Asia

It is from Central Asia that the oldest evidence of the art of knotted rugs has come. First of all, there are the remains of a rug with a geometric design, tied in the Turkish knot, dating from the first century A.D., that were unearthed by the Turfan expedition to eastern Turkestan. Afterward, in the region of Altai, the almost perfectly preserved Pazyryk rug was discovered; it dates from the fourth century A.D. and shows unmistakably the general direction of the style of Central Asian rugs in antiquity. In addition to this marvelous specimen of Turkish knotting, Turkish archaeologists have found the remains of an extraordinarily fine rug tied in the Persian knot in another mound in Altai (Bashadar); in a number of tombs they have found woven rugs and felt rugs with an ingenious variegated coloring for ornamentation. The technical and artistic perfection of all these finds indicates a still longer past in the art of the rug and at the same time explains the admirable artisanry and artistic purity of the rugs of the nomadic Turkomans, preservers of the ancient tradition right into our own days.

Up until about the end of the nineteenth century, there was little information on the rugs of Central Asia because the region was almost totally isolated from the rest of the world. The Turkoman rugs of western Turkestan, made at home by nomads or villagers, were at one time destined solely for personal domestic use. There was also, certainly, some production set aside for exporting to the cities of eastern Turkestan, but this production was earmarked exclusively for China. The regular delivery of Bokhara and Samarkand rugs to Europe did not begin until after China annexed eastern Turkestan and Russia annexed western Turkestan in 1885. Some specimens were left over from the seventeenth and eighteenth centuries. No older ones are known. If, however, we have been able to reconstruct the art of knotted rugs in the past centuries of Central Asia, it is because the old style of Central Asia has been epitomized in the various primitive Seljuk and Ottoman rugs still extant. The Turkoman ornaments on rug fragments of the thirteenth century discovered at Fostat (Old Cairo) are characteristic in this

Rug weaving among the nomads. *Somewhere in the steppes of Hazara two Kurds weave a striped rug. This simple installation, which can be set up only in the open air for making rather large pieces, is unchanged from the original design going back centuries. The nomads and peasants still use it today. It consists of two wooden beams to which the warp threads are attached and kept under horizontal tension by ropes and stakes driven into the earth. The transverse pieces hang from the elevated beam. Attached by slipknots to alternate warp threads, the transverse pieces make it possible to separate the warp threads for the passage of the woof. The same sort of horizontal loom is used to make very finely knotted rugs such as, for example, the Bokharas (see illustration on page 104).*

sense, just as are the rugs with geometric animals of the fourteenth century whose octagonal division of the field resembles the Afghan rugs of the Turkomans. Likewise, the primitive Ottoman rugs of the fifteenth and sixteenth centuries have the same staggered alignment of octagons and lozenges as the well-known Bokhara rugs of the Tekke-Turkomans. However, while at Ushak an arrangement in arabesques of variegated flowers and leaves in the octagons and rhombuses was being developed, the ornaments of the Turkoman rugs remained traditionally geometric. In the pre-Islamic period of Turkestan, animal figures, floral elements, and principal geometric forms were undoubtedly used in combination, as in the Pazyryk rug. The tendency to the purely geometric concept of the design of the rug and to the limitation of the coloring to predominantly red and dark blue—replacing the old polychrome tradition that can be seen in more than one antique Turkoman—seems to be the result of the long isolation of Turkestan and the puritanic influence of the Sunnite Muslims.

Western or Russian Turkestan is the region situated to the east of the Caspian Sea and which today is composed of five Soviet republics. Rugs are made throughout the area, but above all in Turkmenistan by the Ersari, Salor, Saryk, Tekke, and Yomud tribes of Turkomans as well as by the Kirghiz and Baluchi tribes. The members of these tribes are either nomadic herdsmen or small settled peasantry, according to the structure of the country. Their range extends also into the northern parts of Iran and Afghanistan. Since antiquity, all the rugs have been woven and knotted on the horizontal loom of the nomads. Occasionally the rugs are of large size (for example the Afghan and Beshir rugs), but more often they are smaller, in the format of throws and entryway rugs of almost square di-

mensions. Generally, the Persian knot is used; the only exceptions are in the rugs of the Yomud-Turkomans, who frequently use the Turkish knot, and the Kirghiz, who invariably use it. The base fabric is always wool. Nevertheless, at times goat hair is used for the warp of some types. The pile of antique rugs is close-cut and tight, like velour (4 to 6 millimeters); that of new rugs varies from medium-deep to deep (6 to 10 millimeters). Consequently, the structure may be thin and pliable or tight, indeed, at times (when the warp is of goat hair), hard and stiff. Obviously, there are many differences of quality in the structure according to type, origin, and age. The Turkomans call all the main motifs of their rugs *gul* ("flower") and the small ornaments *gülcha* ("floweret").

Afghan rugs are generally made by the Ersari- and Saryk-Turkomans, who occupy northern Afghanistan. The ornamentation consists of large octagons (*guls*) on a brownish-red field in a brick order of three to five rows staggered with arabesques in lozenges, polygons, or much smaller stars. At the center of the octagons there is a polygon filled with stylized plants; other vegetative motifs (the clover leaf, cherry blossoms) appear in the alternately colored quarters of the octagon. Each diagonally opposite pair of quarters has the same base color—orange-yellow, light red, dark blue, natural white. The border

Afghan octagon

100

Ersari-Turkoman (Afghan) rug. *Northern Afghanistan, twentieth century, 304 by 225 centimeters. Warp: goat hair. Woof: wool and goat hair. Pile: wool, 7 millimeters. Density of knotting: 96,000 Persian knots per square meter. Structure: tight, medium-heavy, somewhat hard and ribbed. Such Afghan rugs in vegetable colors are made by the Ersari nomads and the Saryk-Turkomans in the steppes of northern Afghanistan. They differ considerably from the thick Afghan rugs most recently produced in aniline reds.*

Ersari-Turkoman (Afghan) rug. *Northern Afghanistan, beginning of twentieth century, 244 by 140 centimeters. Warp: goat hair. Woof: wool. Pile: wool, 5 to 7 millimeters. Density of knotting: 88,000 Persian knots per square meter. Structure: stiff, medium-heavy, ribbed.*

encloses small lozenges, rectangles, or other geometric forms arranged with a complementary design. An invariable characteristic is the inner border with twining flowers forming a sort of wave. In the same arrangement additional motifs and accessory decorations can be found. With the dominant red field, the dark-blue and brown outlines, and the contrasting colors of the ornaments, the coloring of these rugs is striking. The Afghan rugs that are mass-produced today in Iran and Afghanistan, with their deep pile and chemically derived ox-blood red, share only the design with the now rare Afghan products of the nomads, which, on their close-cut pile, exhibit a warm brownish red and always a bit of light blue and green in the ornamentation. Generally, Afghan rugs are found as runners or are almost square in shape. The side edgings may be flat or rounded and wrapped with goat hair, while woven, striped fabric appears at the two ends. All types are knotted on a warp of goat hair in Persian knots ranging from 80,000 to 140,000 knots per square meter (see illustrations on pages 101 and 110).

Bokhara rugs are produced by the Tekke-Turkomans, who as herdsmen or as seminomadic peasants represent the most powerful Turkoman tribe of the past two centuries. The Tekke rugs known as Bokharas, now also manufactured in Iran by tribal families who have settled there, are the finest and most beautiful rugs of Turkestan, and according to more than one view, the most perfect of all knotted rugs. They were given the name Bokhara, as well as Bokhari, after the geographical designation of western Turkestan; but the name is also generally given to Yomud rugs. The quality of the structure and the thickness of the Tekke and Yomud rugs reminds one of fine animal pelts. The quality is based on a technical characteristic that involves the use of

a lightly twisted warp thread and very fine woof threads; as a result, each row of particularly close knots is tightly beaten down against the previous row. On the smooth, reverse side of the rug, the knots appear to be the fine stitches of a woven fabric. The number of knots can be counted only with great difficulty, and their great density makes it possible to render in detail the most delicate mosaics in the geometric ornamentation of these rugs. The rather small octagonal motifs (*guls*) of the Tekke, somewhat ovalized in form

Octagon of the Tekke-Turkomans, Bokhara

and wavy in contour, are characteristic of these rugs. They are arranged in brick or tile fashion with four to eight rows on the red field. A network of fine lines running lengthwise and crosswise, at the intersections of which the *guls* are placed, indicates the checkerboard pattern of the field. The Tekke-Gul rugs are divided into light and dark quarters and have a central geometric motif from which issue dozens of stylized flowerets alternating with staggered rows of small starry motifs in lozenge form. In the border there is a row of octagonal rosettes separated by serrated leaves and small ornaments. The coloring is very diversified. Generally the field—and invariably the border—is a coppery red or violet, but it is also frequently brick red or a lighter rust red. The ornamentation of antique pieces contains considerable gold-yellow, orange, ruby red (often in red silk), as well as light blue and

Weaving a rug in a Turkoman yurt. *The yurt, a felt-covered trellis of wood with a dome, is the tent of the nomads in the environs of Gonbad-i-Kabus in the northeast portion of Iran. This is the oldest method of making woven or knotted rugs. This horizontal loom set on the ground is still in common use. While working, the weavers are seated on a plank set under the rug, and work bent over the warp threads. This is the way in which Turkoman women weave even the finest rugs, the Bokharas. The Afshar, Qashqai, Kurdish, Lur, and Bergamo rugs, among others, are made in the same way (see illustration on page 92).*

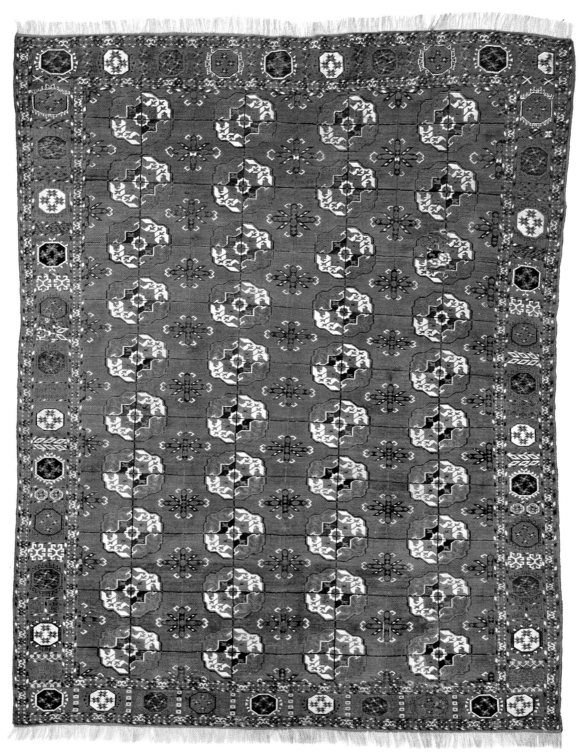

Tekke-Turkoman (Bokhara) rug. *Turkmenistan, western or Russian Turkestan, early nineteenth century, 235 by 193 centimeters. Warp and woof: wool. Pile: wool, 6 millimeters. Density of knotting: 315,000 Persian knots per square meter. Structure: smooth and velvety, dense, delicate, and supple. Antique Turkoman rug like this one frequently have relatively light coloring with multicolored ornaments in the gul motifs and in the narrow border, which has the same color as the field.*

green and contrasting colors and dark-blue and brown outlines. Today, such differently colored Tekke rugs in light tones are rare. A rather uniform and dark red-blue-white coloring now dominates. The smallest rugs often tend toward square shapes. Recently, Bokhara rugs of all sizes and even of runner proportions have appeared on the market. But they are not made by the Tekke-Turkomans. The once short and velvety pile (4 to 6 millimeters) has become noticeably deeper (6 millimeters) in the new examples. The knotting density ranges from 360,000 to 600,000 Persian knots per square meter (see illustration on opposite page).

Beshir (Ersari-Beshir) rugs possess the most richly diversified ornamentation of all the Turkoman rugs. They come from the Amu-Daria region of the ancient emirate of Bokhara. They have been made by the Ersari-Turkomans in the region, often to the order of the city of Bokhara. They are found in long rectangles running to 274 by 732 centimeters. Antique Beshirs exhibit a continuous, repeated design consisting of Herati motifs with stiff tendrils, palmettes, rosettes, and leaves or sinuous cloud ribbons. They generally have a central octagonal medallion with an octagon in each corner. These types are known as Herati Beshirs and "ribbon Beshirs." Other types have stylized tendrils forming a network in lozenge design with palmettes and rosettes. Just as common are those that divide the field in squares or lozenges filled with geometric motifs as well as staggered motifs. The ornamentation of the borders consists of flowers stylized in palmettes or in alignment with various geometrical compositions. A strong brick red dominates the coloring, sometimes as the color of the field but more generally as the principal color of the thickly scattered ornaments on a dark-blue field and set off from it by yellow outlines. The

medium-deep pile is on a base fabric of wool (often with the warp in goat hair), with an average of 120,000 Persian knots per square meter. Beshir prayer rugs (namaslik) have a special beauty. In the niche we find a stylized tree whose hanging branches are trimmed with flowers or pointed leaves (see illustration on page 108).

Ersari rugs are produced in large numbers by the Ersari-Turkomans in northern Afghanistan. Perhaps their ancestors formerly made—as their Beshir rugs seem to indicate—the classical Herati rugs. The *guls* of the Ersari are flattened octagons, with the corners occupied by strongly stylized, horizontal "little firs" or by animal figures so simplified as to take on the form of the letter H. These motifs are arranged in checkerboard pattern and alternate with small, lozenge-shaped stars. The Ersari rugs having these ornaments are called "Afghan" or "Kisil-Ajak" the name of one of the Ersari tribes). The coloring is principally brick or rust red, with dark blue, brown, cream-white, and touches of other colors. Ersari rugs may be found in all shapes. The knotting is average to coarse.

Salor rugs belong to the finest, most beautiful and stylistically pure Turkoman works. They are made by the remnants of the ancient Salor tribe that survived the wars with the Tekke-Turkomans. They have settled in Turkmenistan along the banks of the Murghab and partially in Afghanistan along the Amu-Daria. The *guls* of the Salors consist of a somewhat flattened octagon with a stepped or notched outline surrounded by a crown of geometric arabesques; that is, some of the larger steps end in double pothooks. The same motifs also appear within the octagon itself, turned toward the center, which is occupied by a small octagon. These designs are arranged in a checkerboard fashion in

Beshir carpet (Ersari-Herati-Beshir). *Russian Turkestan or North Afghanistan, mid-nineteenth century. 315 x 160 centimeters. Warp: goat hair. Woof: wool and goat hair. Pile: wool, 4/6 millimeters high. Density of knotting: 126,000 Persian knots per square meter. Structure: very flexible, somewhat reped and hard (brittle). The Beshir is one of the types of Turkmen carpets that have been relatively rare for decades.*

Beshir (Ersari-Beshir) rug. *Turkmenistan, western or Russian Turkestan, nineteenth century, 266 by 140 centimeters. Warp and woof: wool with goat hair. Pile: wool, 6 millimeters. Density of knotting: 134,000 Persian knots per square meter. Structure: dense, tight, somewhat ribbed and granular. Rosettes with a diamond center and arranged diagonally, and small rosettes in the added borders, make up an ornamentation full of style.*

(Right) Salor-Turkoman (Shoval) tent bag. *Turkmenistan, western or Russian Turkestan, nineteenth century, 117 by 76 centimeters. Warp: goat hair. Woof: wool. Pile: wool, 5 millimeters. Density of knotting: 372,000 Persian knots per square meter. Structure: smooth, velvety, thick, and lightly ribbed. Turkoman tent bags consist of a frequently finely knotted front panel and a woven rear panel.*

(Left) Salor-Turkoman (also called Punjdeh or Pindeh) rug. *Turkmenistan, western or Russian Turkestan, nineteenth century, 185 by 122 centimeters. Warp and woof: wool. Pile: wool, 6 millimeters. Density of knotting: 440,000 Persian knots per square meter. Structure: smooth and velvety, delicate, dense, and pliable. The ornamentation offers three rows of Salor guls with a crown of geometric arabesques in a staggered arrangement with smaller Saryk guls. In the added end borders, leaf motifs in the form of combs are arranged on the bias.*

Saryk-Turkoman (Afghan) rug. *Northern Afghanistan, twentieth century, 232 by 115 centimeters. Warp: goat hair. Woof: wool and goat hair. Pile: wool, 7 millimeters. Density of knotting: 92,000 Turkish knots per square meter. Structure: tight, medium-heavy, a bit hard and granular.*

three to five rows staggered with smaller octagons or with rosettes in a lozenge shape. This pattern is to be seen both on throw rugs and on long runners. The coloring is a dark violet-red with orange-yellow, cream-white, and dark blue in the motifs. The borders are often composed of numerous stripes in mosaic motifs. In addition, Salor rugs always have added borders at the two ends, occupied by lozenges. The short pile is like a velour on a base fabric of wool and is made up of about 500,000 Turkish knots per square meter (see illustration on page 109).

The Saryk rugs made by the Turkomans of the same name in the province of Punjdeh (Turkmenistan) and northern Afghanistan are decorated with stepped, flattened octagons that could be described as having added elements on two sides (wings). Generally, in the center there is a lozenge or a hexagon with a cross formed of four stylized flowers. Inside, it is arranged in mosaic fashion and divided by color, in three or four checkerboard rows staggered with small, similar stepped octagons. The border bands are occupied by a particularly rich abundance of motifs. The coloring is dominated by violet-red in the field and brick red in the ornaments, with dark blue, white, and brown as contrasting colors. These rugs are also called Pindeh. The Saryks of Afghanistan frequently have the Ersari *gul* for ornamentation, or also, stepped polygons in staggered rows with small hooked arabesques. The decoration of the borders, the coloring, and the structure have the characteristics of Afghanistan rugs. On the other hand, the Pindeh Saryk rugs have some of the elements of the motifs in ruby-red silk as well as cotton knotting for the parts in white. Generally, all the types are found as throw rugs and long runners. The pile is of medium depth and knotted on a base fabric of

wool with 120,000 to 250,000 Turkish or Persian knots per square meter (see illustration on page 109).

The Yomud rugs of the Yomud tribes have an importance equal to that of the Tekke rugs (Bokharas), while being differentiated from them by their generally heavy structure, a more vigorous coloring, and above all, by an ornamentation based on a lozenge-shaped division of the field. The Yomud-Turkomans inhabit the southeast shore of the Caspian Sea, the region around Khiva, and the countryside near the Atrek and Gurgan rivers is northeast Iran. Yomud rugs have an ornamentation based on reticulated rhombuses. The most beautiful type has lozenge-

Yomud lozenge or diamond motif

shaped forms made up of small lattices with stylized flowers (*kepes-gul*) in a staggered formation. The hooked lozenge (*dirnak-gul*), however, composed of latch hooks similar to geometric branches, always in a staggered arrangement, is the dominant pattern. The ornaments and central elements have various arrangements of form and color in combination, with a light and dark blue, brown, white, and sometimes also green and yellow. There are types with simple lozenges or smooth-sided octagons as well as others in which the lozenges alternate with other decorative motifs. Most often, the cream-colored border is decorated with leaves curled into a spiral and geometric rosettes on a geometric, hooked-wave pattern. Invariably, related bands with a differ-

111

Yomud-Turkoman Rug. *Turk-menistan, western or Russian Turkestan, nineteenth to twentieth centuries, 290 by 185 centimeters. Warp: wool. Woof: wool and goat hair. Pile: wool, 6 millimeters. Density of knotting: 176,000 Turkish knots per square meter. Structure: tight, somewhat ribbed and granular.*

The kepes-gul, *arranged in lozenge-shaped division on this rug, generally is made in several colors that are alternated. The* kepes-gul *motif is the same as the wheat-sheaf motif. The sides and the added end borders have different ornaments.*

Yomud-Turkoman rug. *Turk-menistan or northeastern Iran, twentieth century, 310 by 207 centimeters. Warp and woof: wool. Pile: wool, 8 millimeters. Density of knotting: 210,000 Persian knots per square meter. Structure: smooth, full, pliable, medium-heavy. This type of Yomud, with its lozenge-shaped division, has the* dirnak-gul *design with latch hooks. The white border has an alignment of* achik *rosettes in an arabesque movement, and the added end borders have stylized flowers.*

Yomud carpet (Jamut-Djafarbai). *Turkmenistan, in Russian Turkestan, nineteenth century. 250 x 126 centimeters. Warp and woof: wool. Pile: wool, 7 millimeters high. Density of knotting: 232,000 Turkish knots per square meter. Structure: somewhat grainy and reped, flexible like velvet, almost light. Here three Yomudic gul motifs are divided into five cross stripes and separated from each other by seven narrow stripes.*

ent ornamentation are added to the ends. A brown-red or dark-violet field dominates the few hues in the coloring. Yomuds are found as rectangular throws, medium-size rugs, long runners, and almost square rugs. They have a pile of medium depth, with 180,000 to 320,000 Turkish or Persian knots per square meter (see illustrations on pages 112, 113, and 114–115). Yomud prayer rugs with the niche indicated by a quad-

rangular gable with a small *mihrab* above it are characteristic. The vertical bands of the field contain stylized ascending plants, symbol of the tree of life (see illustration below).

The Chaudor rugs of the Chaudor-Turkomans of the region of Khiva strongly resemble the Yomud rugs both in technique and in style and coloring. The ornamentation of the antique rugs consists of a lozenged division of the reticu-

Yomud (Yomud-Namaslik) prayer rug. *Turkmenistan, western or Russian nineteenth century, 135 by 115 centimeters. Warp and woof: wool. Pile: wool, 6 millimeters. Density of knotting: 220,000 Turkish knots per square meter. Structure: dense, smooth, pliable. A characteristic nomad prayer rug with a quadrangular gable on which is placed a small* mihrab. *In the vertical bands of the field are stylized ascending plants, symbol of the tree of life.*

Chaudor-Turkoman (Chaudor) rug. *Turkmenistan, western or Russian Turkestan, nineteenth century, 125 by 92 centimeters. Warp and woof: wool. Pile: wool, now 4 to 5 millimeters. Density of knotting: 166,000 Turkish knots per square meter. Structure: thin, light, granular. Chaudor rugs belong stylistically to the Yomud rugs, particularly in the ornamentation of their added borders.*

lated field in which variegated *ertman-gul* motifs are aligned. The principal motif is a lozenge with paired latch-hook extensions and various designs inside it, which alternates in staggered rows with smaller rhombuses. The most recent types have hooked rhombuses in a staggered arrangement, with four stylized flowers. The borders and the added end borders, not to mention the formats, are often close relatives of those of Yomud rugs (see illustration above).

The Kachli (Enessi) rugs are the knotted "valances" of the tents of nomadic Turkomans. *Kachli* means "cross," and the name indicates that the field of these small and generally fine

117

Saryk or Kisil-Ajak (Enessi, commonly called Kachli) tent-flap rug. *Turkmenistan, western or Russian Turkestan, nineteenth century, 190 by 135 centimeters. Warp: goat hair. Woof: wool. Pile: wool, 6 millimeters. Density of knotting: 184,000 Persian knots per square meter. Structure: light, somewhat hard and ribbed. This type of Kachli, of distinctly architectural inspiration, shows in the two upper fields of the cross division stylized mosque façades with minarets, and in the lower fields two complex prayer niches (mihrab).*

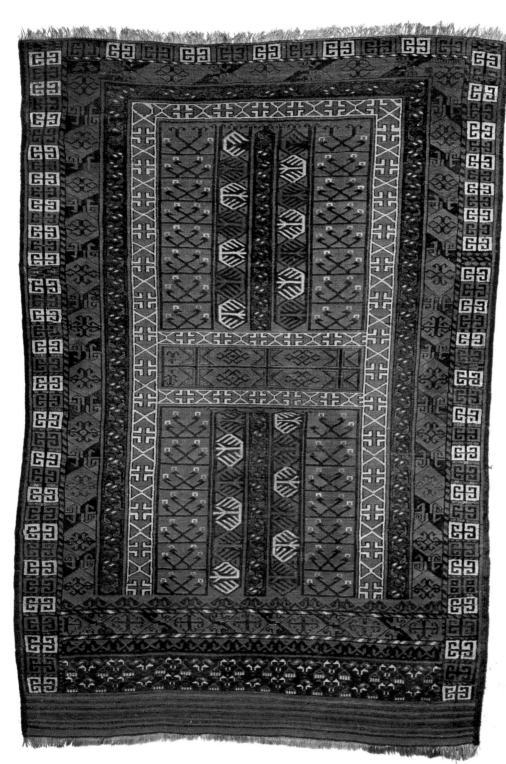

Ersari (Enessi, known as Kachli-Afghan) tent-flap rug. *Northern Afghanistan, nineteenth century, 170 by 115 centimeters. Warp: wool with goat hair. Woof: wool. Pile: wool, now 4 to 5 millimeters. Density of knotting: 102,000 Persian knots to the square meter. Structure: thin, granular, ribbed, somewhat hard. This small-size rug is a Turkoman specialty. It is not used to cover the ground but as a curtain across the tent opening.*

Yomud (Yomud-Enessi, commonly called Kachli) tent-flap rug. *Turkmenistan, western or Russian Turkestan, nineteenth century, 160 by 135 centimeters. Warp and woof: wool. Pile: wool, 6 millimeters. Density of knotting: 224,000 Turkish knots per square meter. Structure: smooth, dense, with a fine grain. Stylized flowers in a field divided into four parts; a row of Yomud palmettes alternately opposed in the two added end borders. The once-variegated coloring has faded as a result of what is called "English washing."*

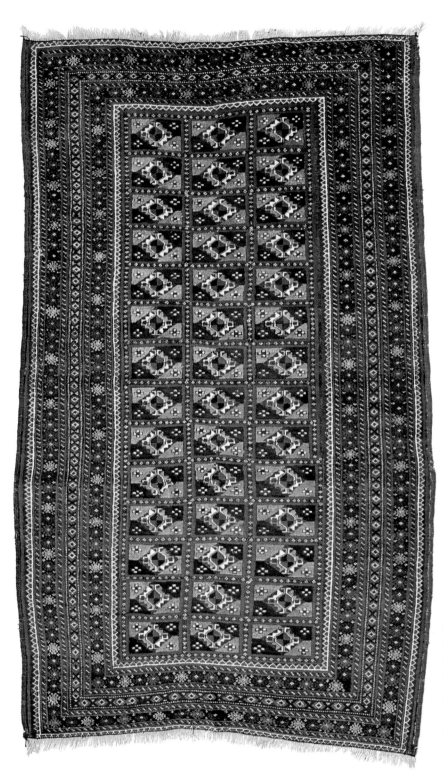

Baluchi (Turkoman-Baluchi) rug. *Border region of Iran and Turkmenistan, nineteenth century, 180 by 105 centimeters. Warp and woof: wool. Pile: wool, 7 millimeters. Density of knotting: 304,000 Persian knots per square meter. Structure: smooth, dense, fine, pliable. The ornamentation is obviously almost entirely Turkoman.*

knotted pieces is divided into four areas by the crossed arms. Frequently niche forms (*mihrab*) are introduced into the vertical bands and in the border above the field, indicating that they were also used as prayer rugs. Stylized calyxes or floral ornaments in rows or in staggered lozenges cover the field. The border is decorated with toothed leaves in pairs and with lozenges, the outer border with characteristic double hooks in white rectangles, and the added end borders with stylized flowers. There are different Kachlis corresponding to the Ersari, Tekke, Kisil-Ajak, and Yomud styles but which the Turkomans always call, without distinction, Enessi. Ornamentation, coloring, structure, and knotting generally correspond to the other products of the tribes (see illustrations on pages 118, 119, and 120).

Baluchi rugs have an abundance of particularly rich motifs and variable ornamentation. The Baluchi nomads move about in the areas of Khorassan, Afghanistan, and Turkmenistan. This explains the diversity of ornamentation and the similarity of their rugs to those of the Turkomans. Since they are nomadic herdsmen, the Baluchis make rugs only in small formats. Nevertheless, they also knot room-size rugs and throws. The generally dark coloring of the ornamentation consists essentially of geometric forms in a staggered or diagonal arrangement as well as in motifs of leaves and strongly stylized flowers. The reticulated division of the field by means of rectangles or rhombuses occupied by various motifs, staggered hexagons or octagons, as well as large, grouped geometric forms, is characteristic of the Baluchis. The Afghan, Bokhara, and Beshir designs are also used. To these must be added those rugs with a geometric medallion, auxiliary elements and corners occupied by designs. The most frequent decoration of the borders is the hooked-wave arabesque, but

there is also a whole series of delicately arranged border ornaments. The severe red-blue coloring with a frequently deep-violet shimmer makes one think of Turkoman rugs. The close to medium-high pile is knotted on a base fabric of wool with an average of 130,000 Persian knots per square meter, though some types frequently attain as many as 360,000 knots. Baluchi prayer rugs have a niche formed of a rectangular gable, and the field is occupied by a leafy tree of life or some stylized plant. Above the niche are two rectangles bearing human hands or a stylized plant. Baluchi rugs are also known under the names Kuduani-, Afghan-, Turkoman-, and Meshed-Baluchi, according to the place where they are made (see illustrations on pages 121, 123, and 124).

The Kirghiz rugs of western and eastern Turkestan (the region of Kara-Kirghize) rarely reach the West and are included in one of the other groups. The ornamentations of the short room rugs consists of a division of the field by decorated, smooth-sided rectangles or lozenges. On the other hand, that of square passageway rugs has an arrangement of three grouped rectangles of somewhat heavy but striking motifs that represent tendrils, flowers, and cloud formations, as well as the old symbols. Angular, hooked arabesques, geometric rosettes, and stepped lozenges are used to decorate the borders. The coloring contains tones of brown-red, dark blue, brown, orange, and natural white. Style and technique are closely linked to those of the Caucasian Kazak rugs. The medium-deep, somewhat shaggy pile is knotted on a base fabric of wool, with about 90,000 Turkish knots per square meter (see cover illustration).

Eastern or Chinese Turkestan (today Sinkiang Uighur) is the desert region (Takla Makan) situated between western Turkestan

Baluchi (Meshed-Baluchi) rug. *Iran, northern region of Khorassan, twentieth century, 176 by 128 centimeters. Warp: cotton. Woof: wool. Pile: wool, 7 millimeters. Density of knotting: 206,000 Persian knots per square meter. Structure: smooth, tight, pliable. The geometric medallion with added elements is emphasized by the corner designs and surrounded by a fine decorative border.*

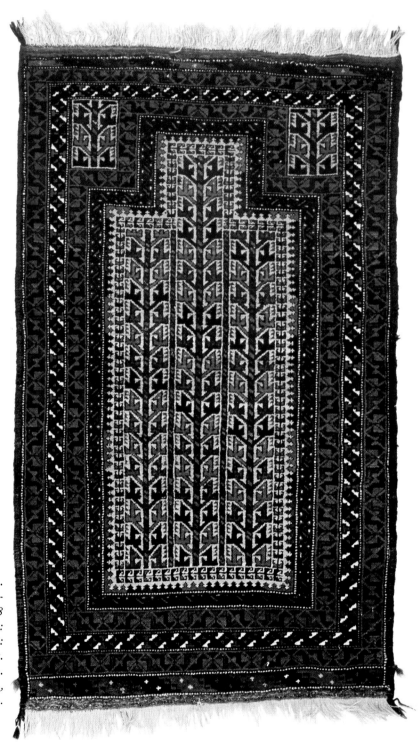

Baluchi (Baluchi-Namaslik) prayer rug. *Border region of Iran and Turkmeni-stan, twentieth century, 128 by 78 centimeters. Warp and woof: wool. Pile: wool, 6 millimeters. Density of knotting: 236,000 Persian knots per square meter. Structure: smooth, dense, light, pliable. In the niche with a typical squared gable, stylized plants suggest the tree of life.*

Kirghiz rug. *Eastern Turkestan, nineteenth century, 190 by 140 centimeters. Warp and woof: wool. Pile: wool, 6 to 7 millimeters long. Density of knotting: 86,000 Turkish knots per square meter. Structure: full, pliable, rough, and grainy.*

Khotan (Samarkand) rug. *Eastern or Chinese Turkestan, now Sinkiang Uighur, nineteenth century, 210 by 100 centimeters. Warp: cotton. Woof: cotton and wool. Pile: wool, 10 millimeters. Density of knotting: 92,000 Persian knots per square meter. Structure: thick, full, soft, granular. This Khotan is ornamented with the so-called box gul decoration in a checkerboard division of the field. In the border is the yun-tsai-tou symbol, which is composed of a large cloud, a ram's horn, and a cloud band. The ornamentation of the field is closely related to a variant of the Gendja rugs of the Caucasus (see illustration on page 60).*

Yarkand or Khotan (Samarkand) rug. *Eastern or Chinese Turkestan, now Sinkiang Uighur, nineteenth century, 234 by 120 centimeters. Warp: cotton. Woof: cotton and wool. Pile: wool, 9 millimeters. Density of knotting: 96,000 Persian knots per square meter. Structure: thick, full, soft, ribbed. The ornamentation of branches and pomegranates in a lozenge arrangement is one of the most beautiful to be found. The border has an arabesque meander and the characteristic swastika rosettes.*

and China, including the Tarim basin, where the old oasis cities of Kashgar, Khotan, Yarkand, etc., are located. Rugs were already being produced there in antiquity, and the fragments found by the Turfan expedition, with their coarse Turkish knots and variegated geometric motifs, demonstrate the character of the Kirghiz rugs. According to Chinese accounts, the art of knotting rugs was practiced in the "agricultural colonies" during the Middle Ages. Huge show rugs—under the influence of Herat—appeared in the eighteenth century and after. They were decorated in the Herati style in brocaded silks. The rugs known since the end of the nineteenth century as Samarkand or Kansu rugs—produced by the Turki population of eastern Turkestan—are stylistically the closest to the Caucasian rugs.

Kashgar rugs are generally long in shape, with a repeated ornamentation stemming from Herati design and consisting of naturalistic tendrils and flowers. Some more recent examples have a series of rather large squares containing octagons outlined in yellow, with blue cloud bands (comparable to the Kazak "cloud-band rugs"). There are types with three rows of squares with blue circles on a yellow ground or yellow-green arabesque wreaths on a red ground. The borders are decorated with rosettes, wave patterns, and flowers, as well as bright herringbone meanders bearing the swastika rosette. Kashgar rugs have a cotton warp and a woolen woof. The woolen or silk pile is medium-deep,

with some 120,000 Persian knots per square meter.

Khotan rugs are also produced in the Herati style with repeated designs of special formation whose ornamentation consists of small lozenges and flowering branches with rosettes of flowers in threes or fives. The motifs are in light blue, rose, yellow, brown, and white on a red field. Simpler types have three circular blue medallions occupied by variegated rosettes on a red or yellow field with grids in the corners. There are types in which the field is covered with a quadrille in two or four rows, with large flowers, and framed in hooked bands in an octagon. This ornamentation is called "box *gul*" (which should be compared with Gendja rugs in this style). But there are also types that have large flowers forming a repeated staggered or diagonal style. Those Khotan rugs whose ornaments consist of small vases arranged in an ascendant pattern, of branches with pomegranates extending into a network of arabesques in the field, of flowers and leaves, have a special beauty (the "pomegranate-branch" design). The borders are decorated with meanders or a major motif of clouds and of cloud-band motifs. The coloring of the Khotan rugs, which are generally long, is gay and lively, composed of only four or five fresh colors. The deep pile (sometimes measuring 12 millimeters), on a base fabric of cotton, numbers 90,000 to 120,000 Persian knots per square meter (see illustrations on pages 126 and 127).

14

Rugs from
Other Sources

The motif of Yarkand rugs is the pomegranate, either on an arabesque of branches or in a network of lozenge shape. Other types have three large medallions in a circle with complementary ornamentation. Aside from these, Yarkand rugs resemble Khotan rugs in all particulars.

Since the middle of the nineteenth century, Chinese rugs have been produced in Peking, Tientsin, and later in Hong Kong exclusively for large-scale export. For a long time the West has taken the rugs produced in eastern Turkestan to be Chinese. But when American and European importers showed an interest in these so-called Kansu rugs, Chinese dealers increased production in the regions that had the necessary wool, especially in the provinces of Sinkiang and Kansu and then in Ningsia, Suiyuan, and Paotow. Workshops were set up in which imitation Khotan rugs were made, as well as a new type with Chinese decorative forms. These are characterized by figurative elements generally arranged asymmetrically, as well as medallions and corner ·patterns consisting of round or grilled elements, symbols and coiling dragons. Among the most esteemed motifs are faithfully depicted household objects, landscapes, animals, and vases with flowering branches, which frequently appear in soft tints on a dark-blue or salmon-pink field. There are also antique seat coverings for benches and carriages, exactly like the borderless rugs with columns, and different rugs with pictures designed to be hung or draped over wooden pillars. The new Chinese rugs from Hong Kong, rather heavy and with a deep pile, are marketed in all shapes and sizes and with ornamentation adapted to Western taste. Generally, a central circular ornament is surrounded by motifs of light pastel plants or flowers freely or symmetrically arranged on a light-green or -blue or salmon-pink field. The decoration of the border is frequently conceived as a wreath and with no line of separation. The motifs in deep pile (as much as 15 millimeters) are frequently sheared in order to give the effect of relief. On a base fabric of cotton, with a markedly spaced-out warp and a ribbed structure, these rugs have about 100,000 Persian knots per square meter, invariably made up of four threads (see illustration on page 130).

Except for the "Pu-lo" rugs woven in dark

Chinese rug. *Suiyuan or Paotow, nineteenth century, wall hanging, 178 by 94
centimeters. Warp: finely twisted cotton.
Woof: cotton and wool. Pile: wool, 10
millimeters. Density of knotting: 85,000
Persian knots per square meter across
four warp threads. Structure: soft, thick,
full, loose. A picture rug that possesses
the characteristics of Chinese-made rugs.*

Tibetan(?) rug. *Northern Tibet or eastern Turkestan, Kirghiz region, nineteenth century, 310 by 155 centimeters. Warp and woof: wool. Pile: wool, now 4 to 6 millimeters. Density of knotting: 92,000 Persian knots per square meter. Structure: medium-heavy, ribbed, granular, pliable. The ornamentation of this rug suggests that it could be of Kirghiz production, but the knotting indicates eastern Turkestan. The Tangut tribes of northern Tibet must have made their own rugs by copying the Kirghiz and eastern Turkestan ornamentation. The coloring in a single tone of red is striking.*

red with white flecks, Tibetan rugs show no particular individual traits. However, knotted rugs originating in eastern Turkestan and China or among nomadic Kirghiz tribes—when they were not made by the Tangut tribes of northern Tibet —were used as temple decorations. Some antique specimens have the characteristics of Kirghiz rugs. The small Tibetan rugs on the market today are made by families that have fled to Nepal. Their ornamentation has been borrowed principally from the rugs of eastern Turkestan and China. The medium-deep pile is knotted on a base fabric of cotton with an average of 80,000 Persian knots per square meter (see illustration on page 131).

Pakistani rugs, products of workshops in West Pakistan, are generally exact copies of Turkoman rugs (Pakistani-Bokhara) as well as of Turkish and Caucasian rugs. Knotted on a base fabric of cotton or wool, these rugs come in all shapes and sizes; the pile is rather deep and glossy, and the wool varies in quality. The density varies between 240,000 and 400,000 Persian knots per square meter.

Indian rugs started in imitation of Persian and Turkish rugs; they were produced for the court and served to display the splendors of the Mogul Dynasty (1526–1803), and later became an article of export. About 1600, numerous workshops were already producing also silk rugs with gold brocade, first in Lahore and later in Agra and other cities. During the sixteenth century the production of the so-called Indo-Persian rugs gradually gave way to the purely Indian style. The ornamentation of the field became imaginative if not at times fantastic. Exaggeratedly "naturalistic" and legendary groups made up of trees, flowering shrubs, birds, animals, and figures from myths—all pictorial in concept— appeared in the foreground. Asymmetrical composition, as well as the plastic nuances of the plants, flowers, and beings reproduced, is also characteristic of these rugs. The borders are frequently occupied by palmette masks framing human and animal heads. Others have loose arrangements of flowering shrubs with even the roots depicted. Many antique Indian rugs nevertheless also have staggered plant ornaments consisting of spear-shaped leaves, palmettes, and rosettes or of arabesques forming lozenges with flowers in them. There also exist those with a repeated design, which resemble the Herati and Kirman rugs. The knotting is extremely fine as a rule, but the coloring is less vivid than in the originals. Rugs resembling the Ispahan rugs of Iran are still being produced today in many Indian cities. The knotting of rugs has even been instituted as a prison occupation. These high-quality rugs, which are destined for export, are known as "Indian Penitentiary," "Indo-Ispahan," or "Indo-Kashmir" rugs. The Mirzapur rugs are certainly sold cheaply but are not a good buy with their coarse knotting, light coloring, shaggy pile, and poor quality of wool. Those Indian rugs made to meet the special requirements of Western houses generally are knotted on a base fabric of cotton and have a medium-deep pile. The Persian knot is used, and the knotting itself is of a fineness that surpasses the average.

Index

Page numbers in italics refer to illustrations.

133